To [handwritten] May your Self-fullness be joyful & satisfying! Dr. Sheila Forman

SELF-FULLNESS

The Art of Loving and Caring for Your "Self"

12/1/03

Sheila H. Forman, J.D., Ph.D.

Writers Club Press
San Jose New York Lincoln Shanghai

Self-Fullness
The Art of Loving and Caring for Your "Self"

Published by Writers Club Press
an imprint of iUniverse.com, Inc.

For information address:
iUniverse.com, Inc.
620 North 48th Street
Suite 201
Lincoln, NE 68504-3467
www.iuniverse.com

ISBN: 0-595-00505-5

Printed in the United States of America

This book is dedicated to all the people who let me into their lives to share their joys, their pains, and their struggles.

Thank you.

EPIGRAPH

SELF-FULLNESS: *the art of taking care of one's needs, desires, and dreams in a healthy, productive and constructive way without guilt and without infringing upon the rights of others; to know one's own person, preferences, and boundaries.*

CONTENTS

Part 1
Self-Fullness Explained

Part 2
Self-Fullness Applied

HOW TO USE THIS BOOK

This book is designed to be used in one of two ways. The first way, I refer to as the "All-the-Way-Through" method. This way means you start from the first page and continue to the last— building your SELF-FULLNESS from start to finish.

The second way I call the "Your Pick" method. You pick a chapter than seems most relevant to you and your life and you start there. If you decide to use this method, I strongly suggest that you read Chapter One first anyway. If you are too eager to get started to do so, read Chapter One as soon as possible. I believe that doing so will allow you to apply the SELF-FULLNESS concepts more thoroughly and enhance your experience.

Throughout the book are exercises to help you apply the concepts presented. You can use the spaces provided within the text to write your answers. Or, if you prefer, you can get a journal of your own to record your responses. I urge you to do the exercises as they present themselves. They will help you to define SELF-FULLNESS for yourself and move you along in your journey.

However you decide to use this book, I sincerely hope that you find help in getting to wherever it is you want to go.

PREFACE

For years I have worked with patients who were struggling to come to terms with who they are and what they want out of life. Part of their struggle dealt with identifying what their needs are and how to get them met without hurting others or, even more important to them, without being called "*selfish.*"

One afternoon during a session with a lovely young woman who felt that she could not pursue her dreams because to do so would go against her family's wishes for her and relegate her to the status of a "selfish little girl," I offered the concept of "*self-fullness.*" I suggested that rather than seeing herself as selfish if she pursued her dreams she might try thinking of herself as "*self-full*," of taking care of her "self" in a healthy, constructive fashion. This idea made sense to her. Suddenly, she felt empowered and ready to take on the world and her dreams.

I began using the concept of SELF-FULLNESS with other patients. Almost "magically," they were able to move past themselves and into their lives.

Let me help you do the same. Come with me on your very own journey of SELF-FULLNESS and start living the life you have always dreamed of.

ACKNOWLEDGEMENTS

How do you thank people who change your life? **Self-fullness: The Art of Loving and Caring for Your "Self"** would never have come into being if it were not for the love, encouragement, and support of the following people: my Mom and Dad, Charlotte and Harry; my sister and brother-in-law, Drs. Marilyn and Glenn Jacobowitz; my dear friends Beth Greenberg, Marji Pearson, and Linda Schutzer; the women of GSI; and, last but certainly not least, the women of my Wednesday morning women's group.

To you all, I humbly say *thank you!*

INTRODUCTION

Imagine a life where you are the best you can be. Imagine knowing exactly what you want and what is important to you. Imagine using that knowledge as a "yardstick" against which you assess your options and make your choices. Imagine asking yourself whether a particular act, thought, behavior, or relationship takes you closer to what you want for your life or further away. Imagine being able to always make the choice that moves you closer. This is the promise of SELF-FULLNESS.

SELF-FULLNESS announces your right to feel good. Your right to a happy and fulfilling life. Your right to healthy relationships, satisfying work, and a healthy, trim, fit body. It dares you to express your individuality. It dares you to be yourself. It dares you to be all you can be!

By adopting the philosophy of SELF-FULLNESS you take charge of your life.

Through the process you are about to embark on you will get to know yourself better than you have before. It is an exciting, fulfilling journey that I am confident will change your life.

For most of you this journey will be exciting and fabulous. For others, the journey may at times be difficult. As you venture on this path, thoughts, feelings, and even sometimes painful memories may reveal themselves to you. If this happens, I encourage you to find yourself a competent, qualified counselor to help you sort through these things. I will help you do this by offering information on how to go about finding such a person.

Part One defines SELF-FULLNESS for you and explains the difference between SELF-FULLNESS and its nemesis *"selfishness"*. Part Two applies SELF-FULLNESS to a wide variety of situations and topics starting from how you eat through how to find your ideal career and how to cope with life's stresses. It is a complete guide to living a full satisfying and happy life.

Throughout the book you will find provocative questions and exercises designed to clarify the ideas presented as well as to build the skills inherent in SELF-FULL living. I encourage to "live the questions." Welcome them. Think about them. Ponder them. The more time you are willing to spend on these questions, the more you will get to know the "real" you and the further along you will move in the SELF-FULL-NESS process. Try to have fun with the exercises, as well. Use them as parlor games with your friends. Take them to your therapist as sources of material for you to work on in your therapy sessions. The uses are endless. Let your imagination take you wherever you want to go. And by all means have fun. That's how life is "supposed" to be led, isn't it?

1

SELF-FULLNESS EXPLAINED

1

SELF-FULLNESS EXPLAINED

Welcome to SELF-FULLNESS. After you have finished reading this book and applying its principles, your life will be better than ever. Through the training you are about to undertake you will learn what your needs, goals, and desires are. You will learn how to achieve them without guilt. You will develop the skills necessary to achieve a full and happy life. Some people have referred to the contents of this book as a "life skills manual," almost a "how-to" book for life. I am complimented by those references because in part that is my aim. To give you the skills you need to build your life. Are you ready to get started? Good. Grab your highlighter or pen and let's go!

One brief comment before we actually begin. Please remember that learning about and developing your SELF-FULLNESS is a process. It will take time for you to incorporate the ideas, concepts and suggestions you are about to encounter into your life. Be patient with the process. Take your time. Remember that just a little bit at a time, and, over time you will completely change how you live your life.

Permission to Take Care of Yourself

Let me start by giving you something that you probably have been unable to give yourself. Permission. Permission to take care of yourself. Permission to put yourself first. Permission to meet your needs, your goals and your desires.

There is an expression that you have to love yourself before you can love another. The same is true for caring for someone. You have to be able to take care of yourself before you are able to take care of someone else.

I am reminded of something I have heard dozens of times. It is the airline instruction regarding the use of oxygen masks during an emergency. The instructions are to place your oxygen mask over your face before assisting someone else. On the surface that may sound "selfish." You will breathe while the other person suffers. But if you think about it closely it makes sense. If you do not put your oxygen mask on your face you will not be able to breathe. If you are not breathing what good are you to somebody else? The same is true for SELF-FULLNESS.

SELF-FULLNESS Defined

SELF-FULLNESS is defined as *"the art of taking care of one's needs, desires and dreams in a healthy, productive and constructive way without guilt and without infringing upon the rights of others; to know one's own person, preferences, and boundaries."* If you look in a dictionary for the definition you won't find it. I created *"self-full"* in response to the word *"selfish."*

In the dictionary you will find a definition for *"selfish." "Selfish"* is defined by Webster as *" concerned exclusively or excessively with oneself; arising from concern with one's own welfare or advantage in disregard of others."*

The word *"selfishness"* has negative connotations, even some might say, a negative reputation. To be *selfish* is to act only in your own interest without concern for the health, welfare or feelings of someone else. A *selfish* person is often a lonely person. Who wants to spend time with someone who doesn't care about anyone else? It is for these reasons that so many people fear being labeled *selfish* and consequently live their entire lives putting their needs and desires behind them and focusing their time and energy on others.

In this book I hope to offer you a different approach to life. An approach that allows you to respect yourself and take care of your own needs without fearing that you will hurt others and without thinking of yourself as *selfish*.

Respecting yourself is an underlying premise of SELF-FULLNESS. As we go on you will learn various ways of doing this. Over time respecting yourself will become second nature to you. When that happens you will have arrived at the goal post of SELF-FULLNESS.

Shifting Paradigms

Let us continue with an important *"paradigm"* shift. A *"paradigm"* is a pattern or model that you use to explain and understand the world. For example, let us say that you were raised by an alcoholic mother. You may have defined yourself as "an adult child of an alcoholic" and viewed all of your relationships, issues, and problems through that perspective. That perspective is your paradigm—your way of seeing the world.

Most people who do not take care of themselves or who are afraid to do so because of the repercussions that may occur to them from their family and friends have a "victim" paradigm. They tend to view themselves as powerless. As the victim of their circumstances. As a victim of their life. I do not mean this in a negative or judgmental way. I intend it merely as an observation.

To continue your journey to SELF-FULLNESS, we will begin with a shift in this victim paradigm. From this moment forward, I want you to start seeing yourself as someone who has something to say about your life and your circumstances. As somebody who can do something about them.

Exercise. From Victim to Victorious

1. Identify a situation in which you felt like a victim. A situation where, for example, you said yes to something when you really wanted to say no. Or, where someone took advantage of you.

_____
_____
_____
_____
_____
_____
_____
_____
_____

2. Now rewrite that experience with you acting the way you "wished" you had acted. For instance, rescript the above example so that this time you are saying no.

_____
_____
_____
_____
_____
_____
_____
_____
_____

3. How did you feel as you rewrote history? Did you feel empowered? Less like a victim? More victorious?

_____

_____

_____

_____

_____

_____

_____

_____

_____

Try this exercise with other situations you have come across. The more you practice being "victorious", the easier it will become.

Claiming Your Authority

Did you know that no one has authority over you but you? I am not talking about law and order authority. I am talking about personal authority. The right to decide who you are and how you feel.

Many people, women in particular, feel that they may not have their feelings. They believe that their feelings are wrong or inappropriate or invalid. Often times well-meaning parents or other "grown-ups" say to children "you shouldn't feel that way" or "don't cry." By giving children these messages they are teaching them that who they are and what they feel is wrong. This can set up a pattern of mistrusting or disregarding personal feelings that lasts a lifetime. Does any of this seem familiar to you? Your feelings are your feelings. They are neither right nor wrong. They just are. As are the feelings of other people. Allowing free expression of feelings, in any circumstance, is very emotionally healthy. Start now by giving yourself permission to have your feelings. Reclaim your authority over yourself and your emotional life by acknowledging that

you have the right to feel any feeling you have, even if others believe it
to be "wrong."

Exercise. Claiming My Authority

Here is an exercise to help you regain your authority by reclaiming
your feelings.

1. Identify a situation where you had an emotional reaction to something and were told not to. What were the circumstances? What were
you feeling? Who told you not to have your feelings?

_____

_____

_____

_____

_____

_____

_____

_____

2. Now, give yourself permission to have those feelings. Imagine yourself in that situation again and feel your feelings. If you need to cry, cry.
If you need to shout, shout. You can say your feelings aloud. You can
write them down. You can tell them to someone you trust. How do you
feel? Record your insights here.

_____

_____

_____

_____

_____

_____

_____

Feeling Deserving

Your beliefs have a very tight hold over who you are, how you feel, and what you believe you deserve to have in life. Your belief system, combined with your thoughts, actually create the life you are living. Anything that you currently have in your life began as a belief. Think about it. Where do you live now? Are you in a house or an apartment? When you were looking for a place to live didn't you hold some beliefs about what you could afford or in what neighborhood you wanted to live? Inherent in those beliefs are other underlying beliefs relating to how you feel about yourself and what you feel you deserve. Maybe you see yourself as someone who could never live in a house because you couldn't handle the responsibility. Your belief that you can't handle responsibility keeps you living in an apartment rather than in your dream house.

Exercise. *If You Think You Can or You Think You Can't, You're Right.*

1. Is there something in your life you would like to do or have but believe that for some reason you can't? What is that something?

_____

_____

_____

_____

_____

_____

_____

_____

_____

2. What beliefs do you hold about that something that is convincing you that it cannot be yours?

_____

_____

_____

_____

_____

_____

_____

_____

_____

_____

3. Are those beliefs true? Are they based in reality? Or, are they based in history or fiction?

_____

_____

_____

_____

_____

_____

_____

_____

_____

4. What beliefs would allow you to bring that special something into your life? Would believing that you are deserving of it help? How about a belief that says it is possible to achieve it? Record the beliefs that would help you here.

_____

_____

_____

_____

_____

_____

---

5. Pick one of the affirming beliefs you recorded in step 4 and repeat it to yourself daily. Start convincing yourself that this new belief could be true. Start looking for evidence in your environment to support your new belief. Once it has taken hold, choose another, and so forth until you have adopted a new belief system. Your new belief system will make it possible for that special something of yours to come to you. Use the space below to record how and when your special something came into your life.

The last step of this exercise is an introduction into the use of positive affirmations as a tool for SELF-FULL success. Positive affirmations are statements you say to yourself that are inspirational and uplifting. Their purpose is to "reprogram" your unconscious mind from a negative, life-defeating mind to a positive, life-affirming mind. Positive affirmations can be an effective tool in your SELF-FULLNESS toolbox if you use them to focus your mind and your actions on the things you want to accomplish. Your unconscious mind is a powerful instrument that works hard to bring into your life the things you think about. If you think about negative people and places you will find yourself in those very places. If you think about positive people and places you can have a very different experience. This is not magic. It is actually quite simple. You get what you focus on. For example, if you think about red Toyotas and go out for a drive you will be struck (no pun intended!) by the number of red Toyotas you "suddenly" see. Actually, those red Toyotas were there all the time only this time you were able to "see" them because you were focused on them. If you think there are no good men left in the world, that is exactly what you will see— "no good men." On the other hand, if you practice saying to yourself that there are lots of great men out there you will "suddenly" notice them as never before. Here's an exercise to help you do just that.

Exercise. Positive Affirmations.

1. What negative statements occupy your thoughts?

_____

_____

_____

_____

_____

_____

_____

_____

_____

2. Rewrite those statements into positive, believable statements. For example, if your negative statement is "I'll always be fat," change it to "I'm working on ways to lose weight." Saying that will "allow" you to start seeing ways for you to change how you eat and overtime you will start losing weight. Make sure that these statements are said in the present tense.

_____

_____

_____

_____

_____

_____

_____

_____

_____

3. Choose one of your new positive statements and write it on a sepa-rate piece of paper and hang it where you can see it often. Practice recit-ing the affirmation several times throughout the day. Once this statement becomes "second-nature" to you, choose another one and do the same thing. What new one will you choose?

_____

_____

_____

_____

_____

_____

_____

_____

_____

Learning from Success

Most people who want to change their lives think about the mistakes they have made and try to correct them. I believe that there is a better way to make a change. From my point of view, focusing on your mis-takes, on what you did wrong, is a negative perspective. A perspective that keeps you dwelling in your past and in your pain. I would like to offer you another idea.

Rather than look to your mistakes to learn from, look to your suc-cesses. Your successes teach you much more about what you can do and what works for you. This is a positive affirming perspective. SELF-FULLNESS is about moving forward and being positive. Focusing on your successes is the SELF-FULL way to change.

Ultimately, SELF-FULL success comes from doing what you know is right for you.

Exercise. Learning from Success

1. Recall a time in your life when you succeeded at something. It could be the day you got your driver's license, or the time you asked your boss for a raise and got it. Describe in as much detail as you can what you did that brought about that success.

_____

_____

_____

_____

_____

_____

_____

_____

_____

2. Identify the strengths, resources, and wisdom you used to bring about your favorable results. For example, you tried over and over until you got it—that's persistence. Or, you surfed the web for information on your problem-that's resourcefulness.

_____

_____

_____

_____

_____

_____

_____

_____

_____

3. Give yourself credit for the strengths, resources, and wisdom you have inside you. Acknowledge that you have what it takes to do what you want. Rely on these strengths the next time you are faced with a challenge. I am giving myself credit for:

_____

_____

_____

_____

_____

_____

_____

_____

_____

A Lesson in Values

So what exactly is it that you like? What are your preferences? What matters to you? What are your priorities? If you are new to the SELF-FULLNESS way of life you probably do not know the answers to these questions. That's okay. I am about to help you figure it all out.

To find out the answers, focus on your values. Values answers the question: What matters to you most?

***Exercise.** Figuring Out What Matters*

Part One:

To figure out what matters to you, think about the questions below. There is space provided for you to record your thoughts.

Values at Home

How important is your family to you? Do you feel comfortable with the amount of time you spend together? Do you want more time together or less? Do you enjoy the activities you share? Which activities would you like to add, omit or change? Do you like where you live? Is your home where you want it to be? Would you rather live somewhere else? If so, where?

Write your thoughts here:

_____
_____
_____
_____
_____
_____
_____
_____
_____

Values at Play

Who are your friends? Do you like them? Do you want more friends? How important are your friendships to you? What would you like to change about the friendships you have now? Do you keep up with old friends? Do you want to? Do you want to make new friends? If so, what are you willing to do to make new friends?

Write your thoughts here:

_____
_____
_____

_____

_____

_____

_____

Values at Work

How important is work to you? How important is having a career? What do you want to get out of the work you do? What do you like about your current work? What do you dislike? What would you like to change? Do you work best with others or alone? Do you prefer to be in a leadership position or one of a team? Do you like work that is predictable and stable or creative and risky?

Write your thoughts here:

_____

_____

_____

_____

_____

_____

_____

_____

_____

Values at Your Core

Do you like who you are? What about you do you like? What would you want to change? Do you like change? Do you seek it or avoid it? What can you change? What can you not change? Do you welcome risky, exciting new adventures? Do you feel secure? If not, what would it take to feel secure?

Write your thoughts here:

_____

_____

_____

_____

_____

_____

_____

_____

_____

Values at the Bank

How happy are you with your current financial picture? How much money do you need to live well? Do you feel financially secure? If not, what would it take to feel that way?

Write your thoughts here:

_____

_____

_____

_____

_____

_____

_____

_____

_____

Part Two:

Here is another exercise for you to try to further your understanding of your values.

1. To figure out what your values are take a look at the list of values below. Make a check mark next to the ones that seem to be important to you.

Appearance	Material Possessions	Money
Social Status	Professional Status	Health
Honesty	Integrity	People
Empathy	Trustworthiness	Kindness
Ambition	Discipline	Tenacity
Humor	Strength	Courage
Effort	Intelligence	Determination
Compassion	Sensitivity	Relaxation
Freedom	Independence	Community
Passivity	Action	Risk
Safety	Security	Popularity
Faith	Fame	Thriftiness

2. From the values you marked, pick the ones that describe you the most, or add your own. List them here.

_____

_____

_____

_____

_____

_____

_____

_____

_____

_____

_____

3. Now prioritize your list starting with the value you feel is the most important to you.

From your priority list you have your values. You have what is important to you. You can now use this list to help you make better life decisions. For more on SELF-FULL decision-making see Chapter Twelve.

Self-Perception

One of the benefits of your SELF-FULLNESS journey is that you will really get to know yourself. You will have an accurate assessment of who you are, what you want, and how you seem to others. In other words, you will have a healthy self-perception. The exercise that follows is to be used at least twice in your SELF-FULLNESS quest. Do it now to get an understanding of how you perceive yourself now and do it again later to see how your perception has improved.

Exercise. Who Am I?

Here are a list of questions geared to helping you understand who you are. What will you learn about yourself? Let's find out.

1. Who are you? How would you describe who you are to someone who doesn't know you?

_____

_____

_____

_____

_____

_____

_____

_____

_____

2. What do you believe you can do? Everything? Nothing? Something? What things?

_____

_____

_____

_____

_____

_____

_____

_____

_____

3. How do you see yourself? What kind of person are you? Kind, thoughtful, quiet, out-going?

_____

_____

_____

_____

_____

_____

_____
_____
_____

4. What do you expect of yourself? Lots or not much?

_____
_____
_____
_____
_____
_____
_____
_____
_____

5. What are your strengths? Some examples of strengths are: responsi-ble, organized, productive, open-minded, good at details, coordinated, good communicator.

_____
_____
_____
_____
_____
_____
_____
_____
_____

6. What are your limitations? Some examples of limitations are: criti-calness, judgmentalness, hard to say no.

_____
_____

---

7. What are your goals? Short term? Long term? At work? Personal?

Changing Your Self-Image

In earlier discussions, we talked about how your thoughts and your beliefs influence what you have in your life. Your thoughts and beliefs also influence how you perceive yourself. They create your self-image. In essence, you are who you think you are. Therefore, if you are unhappy with who you are, if you would like to change your self-image, think differently! The previous exercise helped you answer the question: Who are you now? Think about who you want to be. Start in your imagination and see yourself as you wish yourself to be. Practice this daily and soon you will start to become that very person. This is the skill of creative visualization. What you can "see" in your imagination, you can create in your reality.

Eliminating Perfectionism

One of the greatest traps that people fall into is the perfectionism trap. The idea that everything has to be just right before anything else can happen. Perfectionism is actually a defense mechanism. It prevents you from moving forward. It gives the thinker a rationale for why things are not happening. It is all a big lie. Giving up the need to be perfect is probably the biggest step you can take towards achieving SELF-FULL-NESS. Doing so allows you to be yourself and that is what SELF-FULL-NESS is all about.

Living in the Gray

Part of giving up perfectionism is learning to live in what I call "the gray." Perfectionists tend to be black and white thinkers. Everything is either all right or all wrong. Learning to see the gray, the middle ground, the less-than-perfect in a given situation, is a vital part of eliminating perfectionism.

Exercise. Shades of Gray

1. What do you view in your life in terms of black and white? What is either all right or all wrong? Where do you expect perfectionism?

_____

_____

_____

_____

_____

_____

_____

_____

_____

2. What would the "gray" look like in your life? Would you allow your-self to be pleased with less than perfect results on an exam you studied hard for? Would it be okay to have a week on your diet result not in weight loss but rather in better habits, such as passing on the dessert when you went out to dinner?

_____
_____
_____
_____
_____
_____
_____
_____
_____
_____
_____

3. How would "living in the gray" feel to you? Would life be more peace-ful? More joyful? Describe how your life could change if you adopted this new attitude.

_____
_____
_____
_____
_____
_____
_____
_____
_____

Removing Shoulds

Shoulds are obligations imposed on you from the outside. SELF-FULLNESS means asking YOURSELF what needs to be done and doing that. Read on and you'll learn just how to do that.

From an early age, most people, particularly women are conditioned to ignore their inner voice and internal messages. Instead, they are taught to follow an established set of rules known as the "shoulds" and the "ought to's". By relying on these rules, you learn to not trust your own feelings. These "instructions" are passed down from generation to generation. Until now. You have an opportunity to end the tyranny of the "should's" and the "ought to's".

Learning to trust your inner voice is a difficult task for many. Later in the section that follows you will learn ways to make your inner voice stronger. For now, let's take a look at the role that "shoulds" have played in your life so far.

Exercise. I shoulda, woulda, coulda....

1. Have you been the victim of the "tyranny of the shoulds?" If not, consider yourself fortunate. If so, what were the circumstances? What were the consequences?

_____

_____

_____

_____

_____

_____

_____

_____

_____

_____

2. What would you have preferred to do under those circumstances? How would the outcome have changed?

_____
_____
_____
_____
_____
_____
_____
_____
_____
_____

3. What fears do you have associated with letting go of the "shoulds?"

_____
_____
_____
_____
_____
_____
_____
_____
_____

4. What would the benefits be to you by letting go of the "shoulds?"

_____
_____
_____
_____
_____
_____
_____

Trusting Your Instincts

A secret ingredient in this journey is your instincts. Learning to listen to them is the way to SELF-FULLNESS.

Another word for instincts is intuition. Intuition is the equivalent of inner knowing. It can be described as hunches, inspiration, that little voice inside of you, prompting, or nagging feelings. It is that quiet tap on your shoulder. Acknowledge it. It will take you where you want to go.

People who the world consider to be geniuses are those who have had the confidence and courage to listen to and follow the guidance of their intuition. Follow yours . Obey it and you will find joy, peace, satisfaction and SELF-FULLNESS. Ignore it and you will experience confusion, pain, and unhappiness. If you follow your intuition faithfully, you will be led to the result that is right for you.

Learn to listen inwardly and follow your intuitive feelings. The message will be clear if you become quiet and listen for it. An intuitive feeling that is trying to tell you something or someone is not good for you will feel like restlessness, discomfort, or discontentment. You feel as if something is not right but you cannot put your finger on it. An intuitive feeling that is supporting a choice will feel like excitement, joy, energy and peace. The message is clear for you to hear if you become quiet and listen for it.

Observe yourself and your intuition will reveal itself. Honor it and it will guide you to SELF-FULLNESS. Intuition points the way. Here are the two steps you need to take to develop your intuition. First, give your intuition your full attention. Trust your gut reactions. Notice what happens when you follow them. Notice the flow of increased energy and power that you feel. Notice the calmness that over takes you. Second, take a leap of faith and trust that deep down inside you really do know what is best for you. As you learn to trust your intuition, be prepared for surprises. Problems are not always solved in the expected fashion.

Your solutions may seem unusual or especially creative. That's your intuition at work. Record your intuitive findings here.

_____

_____

_____

_____

_____

_____

_____

_____

_____

Your Self-Partnership

In pursuing SELF-FULLNESS, you will be learning to form a partnership with yourself. You will become your own coach. To create this relationship with yourself, start, if necessary, by treating yourself as you would treat someone else. Sometimes it is easier to take care of someone else than to take care of your own self if you are not used to doing so. As you get used to thinking of yourself first, you will be able to take better care of yourself.

By taking responsibility for yourself and taking charge of your life you insure your own well-being. Sadly it is the person who seeks to be taken care of or rescued by another who loses the chance to find success, joy, and happiness.

SELF-FULLNESS and Self-Esteem

Self-esteem is an important component of SELF-FULLNESS. Self-esteem is the opinion you have of yourself. The higher your self-esteem the better you feel about yourself and the more confidence you have in your opinions and choices. The more confidence you have in your opinions and choices, the more confidence you will have in your ability to handle life. The more confidence you have in your ability to handle life, the more SELF-FULL you will become.

To build self-esteem you need to "*do the tough stuff.*" Challenge yourself to build your self-esteem. What are some things you can do? How about training for a marathon? Setting and meeting a goal? Raising money for charity? Starting a business? Taking an auto repair or electronics class? Learning how to do your own taxes?

Exercise. *10 Ways to Raise My Self-Esteem*

In the space below, list ten things you can do to challenge yourself and increase your self-esteem. One you might want to include is learning to accept compliments. (Here's a hint, say "thank you!")

_____
_____
_____
_____
_____
_____
_____
_____
_____

Let me add a word about compliments here. For many people, a compliment is a very hard thing to accept. People are often inclined to negate the compliment with some put-down or dismissal. For example, when Caryn was complimented on a particularly pretty dress, she was very quick to reply " Oh it's not so great. I only paid $15 for it." The SELF-FULL response that Caryn could make in the future would be "Thank you, I like it too."

SELF-FULLNESS and its Affect on Others

Sometimes it is hard to act SELF-FULL because following through is doing something different. Different can be frightening. You may "*rock the boat*" by doing things that others may not like. More often than not, people who are not SELF-FULL themselves are "invested" in keep others from changing. There is comfort in certainty and when someone changes, that certainty erodes. This can cause a great deal of stress for some who may then go to great lengths to maintain the "status quo." We frequently refer to this behavior as "sabotage." In other words, people who are threatened by your changes may try to prevent you from making them. They may act aggressively or passively.

An example of aggressive interference is arguing with you or calling you names when you are doing something they don't like. Passive interference could be coming home late so you cannot leave for your class on time. By doing so, they prevent you from attending your class, which prevents you from changing. They perceive themselves as "innocent" of any wrong doing because they didn't "tell you not to go."

The SELF-FULL way to handle sabotage is to recognize it for what it is and ignore it. Recognize that the behavior is a reflection of the saboteur's insecurities and continue on your way. If your husband for example passively returns late to home on your school night, hire a baby-sitter so his actions don't interfere with your plans. You don't have to make a big deal out of it. Simply say, " I realize that it is hard for you to get home on time for me to leave, so to help us both I have hired a sitter to come and watch the kids until you get home." If you are faced with an aggressive interferer use your assertiveness to acknowledge their position and do your own thing anyway. You will find a lot of help on developing your assertiveness in Chapter Four on SELF-FULL Relationships.

Just a note on extremely difficult sabotage situations. If you find yourself facing extremely hostile and even dangerous behavior in response to your pursuit of SELF-FULLNESS you will need to reevaluate the relationship that is being affected. It may become necessary for you to remove yourself from the relationship if your well-being, physically or emotional, is being threatened. To leave a bad situation is a SELF-FULL action.

SELF-FULLNESS in a Nutshell

So, that's SELF-FULLNESS explained. In the chapters that follow, the concept of SELF-FULLNESS is applied to a wide variety of life circumstances, including nutrition, fitness, relationships, and careers. Read on for some exciting ways to bring SELF-FULLNESS to life.

2

SELF-FULLNESS APPLIED

2

SELF-FULL EATING

Let's Get Started

A great place to start adopting SELF-FULL ideas and skills is in the area of food. Contrary to what you may think you actually have a lot of control over your food choices. In this chapter you will learn exactly how to make those choices. You will learn how to know your "food self" and your preferences. You will become aware of the affect food and drinks have on your body and your emotions. I will show you how to construct a healthy food plan so you can achieve permanent slimness. You will also learn how to eat in a SELF-FULL way in the company of others, without hurting their feelings or stepping on their toes.

Your instincts or intuition that we explored in Chapter One will play an important role in your developing your SELF-FULL way of eating. The key will be in getting to know yourself and your body. The exercises contained in this chapter are designed to help you get in touch with what your body enjoys, what your body needs, what feels good, and what does not. Ultimately eating in the SELF-FULL way will bring you to the weight that is most appropriate for you. In some cases that will mean permanent weight loss.

The things to remember are that knowing what you like to eat and believing that you have the right to the foods you enjoy are the essence of SELF-FULL eating. In learning the lessons that this Chapter offers, you will stop abusing your body by overeating, undereating, or merely poorly eating and achieve the healthful body you were meant to have.

Nourishing Your "Self" the SELF-FULL Way

By nourishing yourself the SELF-FULL way, you will feel better, have more energy and stamina, and better health. So, what exactly does it mean to eat in a SELF-FULL way? It means eating for you and for no one else. It means making healthy food choices so you look and feel better. It means eating only foods that you truly enjoy and that taste good to you. It means saying no to seconds if you are satisfied even if doing so will "insult" your mother-in-law. It means requesting your salad dressing on the side even if doing so "embarrasses" your spouse. Remember Meg Ryan's performance of Sally in the movie "When Harry met Sally?" The restaurant scenes epitomized SELF-FULL eating!

SELF-FULL eating is intuitive eating. It is knowing when you are hungry, what you are hungry for, nourishing your body with those foods, and stopping when your body has had enough. It is instinctual. Getting to know your instincts is an exciting journey. Getting to trust them is empowering. Finally, using them to guide you in your eating is SELF-FULL. When you rely on internal cues to tell you when to eat, what to eat, and when to stop you honor yourself. If you allow your innate wisdom to be in charge and do not interfere with its signals, you will achieve your natural and healthiest weight. We are not shooting for perfection here. One "bad" food, or one excessive meal, or even one binge-filled day will not ruin SELF-FULL eating. We are shooting for an over-all approach to food that is thoughtful and healthy.

Knowledge is Power

The first step in SELF-FULL eating is getting to know yourself and your preferences. If you are like many Americans you have spent most of your adult life dieting. That means you have spent most of your adult life making food choices based on what other people have told you to eat. In an effort to lose unwanted pounds many of you have suffered through meals of foods you do not enjoy. SELF-FULLNESS puts an end to all that. From now on you choose only foods you enjoy. That's not to say you spend the rest of your days only eating chocolate. To do that would be contrary to the concept of SELF-FULLNESS because a diet made up exclusively of chocolate would hurt your health. Instead, SELF-FULL eating offers the idea that everything is edible—just in moderation. More on moderation and its role in SELF-FULL eating coming up. But, first let's continue our work on knowledge and preferences.

Here's an exercise designed to help you get to know your "food self" a bit better.

Exercise. Getting to Know Me and My Preferences.

1. Make a list of all the foods you enjoy whether or not you allow yourself to enjoy them right now.

_____

_____

_____

_____

_____

_____

_____

_____

2. Make a list of the foods you eat right now as part of your current dietary plan.

_____

_____

_____

_____

_____

_____

_____

_____

_____

_____

3. Compare the two lists. How much do they overlap? How much do they differ? When you are eating the SELF-FULL way the two lists will be practically identical.

Record your observations here:

_____

_____

_____

_____

_____

_____

_____

_____

_____

4. For the next five days write down all the foods and drinks you consume. Next to each entry make a note as to whether or not you truly enjoyed that particular food. Did it taste good to you? Was it hot enough? Too hot? Too cold? Start noticing how much food you consume that you truly do not enjoy. Also notice how much of your diet is made up of foods you like.

Day 1:

_____

_____

_____

_____

_____

_____

_____

_____

_____

_____

_____

_____

Day 2:

_____

_____

_____

_____

_____

_____

_____

_____

_____

_____

_____

Day 3:

_____

_____

_____

_____

_____

Day 4:

Day 5:

---

5. Now pull out your first list. The one that listed the foods that you enjoy. Look them over. Have you eaten any of them in the last five days? If so did you enjoy them as much as you thought you would? Sometimes a food that we have denied ourselves for a long time because of some foolish diet rule we were adhering to really isn't a favorite after all. Once you allow yourself to eat all the types of foods you want you may be surprised to discover that after all these years you really prefer vanilla ice cream to chocolate! What did you learn? Record what you learned here.

_____

_____
_____
_____
_____
_____
_____
_____
_____
_____
_____

Now be sure to start including the foods you truly enjoy into your life. You need not fear that if your let, say chocolate, into your life you will eat nothing but chocolate every day for the rest of your life. This fear is known as an "eating backlash." You may do that for awhile but trust me after time when you know in your heart that you can have chocolate whenever you want because you are living the SELF-FULL way the urge to overeat the chocolate will fade and it will become "just another food that you enjoy."

No Longer Now or Never; Instead, Now or Whenever

In essence, what SELF-FULL Eating is giving you is unconditional permission to eat the foods you love. Unconditional permission to eat the foods you love causes the food to lose its power. Why is that? The answer is rather simple. We, as human beings, covet that which we think we cannot have. An object, a person, a food, becomes more desirable when we think we cannot have it. Once we have it, it loses a lot of its attractiveness. Check this out for yourself.

Exercise. Break That Evil Spell

Think about something you once wanted that you thought you couldn't live without and then got it. What happened? Did its spell endure or did you tire of it soon thereafter?

_____

_____

_____

_____

_____

_____

_____

_____

_____

_____

If you are like most people you tired of it or lost interest. The same will happen with food if you let it. Here's a tip: If you do not love it, do not eat. If you do love it, enjoy every luscious morsel of it.

Food and Moods

The next step is becoming aware of the affect of food on your body and your moods. This is important because to be SELF-FULL means to take good care of yourself. If you love the taste of milk, but are lactose intolerant, for example, then drinking milk has a negative effect on your body and your health. The SELF-FULL choice would be to omit milk from your food plan. Another example might be diet soda. Perhaps you love diet soda but discover that it causes your skin to break out. Armed with this information you can make a SELF-FULL decision on whether to include diet soda in your food plan. Awareness leads to information. Information leads to choices. Choices lead to SELF-FULLNESS.

Here is an exercise designed to help you become aware of the affect of food on you.

Exercise. I'm in the Mood for Food

1. For the next five days write down all the food you eat and all the beverages you drink. Next to each entry on your list note how what you ate or drank made you feel. Here are some ideas:

Pay attention to what made you feel happy, feel sad, what gave you a lift, what made you depressed, and what made you feel anxious or nervous.

             Food   Mood

Day 1:

_____

_____

_____

_____

_____

_____

_____

_____

_____

_____

_____

Day 2:

_____

_____

_____

_____

_____

_____

_____

_____

_____

_____

_____

_____

Day 3:

_____

_____

_____

_____

_____

_____

_____

_____

_____

_____

_____

_____

Day 4:

_____

_____

_____

_____

_____
_____
_____
_____
_____
_____

Day 5:

_____
_____
_____
_____
_____
_____
_____
_____
_____
_____

2. Take a look at your entries. Do you notice any patterns? Did you learn anything that surprised you? Are there foods that you may choose to avoid as a result of this exercise? Are there foods you will choose more of ? Write your insights here:

_____
_____
_____
_____
_____
_____
_____
_____
_____
_____

Exercise. Cause and Effects.

This exercise focuses on the physical affects of the food you eat.

1. For the next five days, write down your food and drinks and make a note about the following:

- Which foods give you energy?
- Which foods put you to sleep?
- Which foods give you hives?
- Which foods agree with you? Which foods do not?
- Which foods make you itch?
- Which foods give you a headache?
- Which foods give you a stomach ache?
- Which food leave you feeling full and satisfied?
- Which foods leave you feeling hungry and needing more?

           Food   Physical Reaction

Day 1:

_____

_____

_____

_____

_____

_____

_____

_____

_____

_____

Day 2:

_____

_____

_____

_____

_____

_____

_____

_____

_____

_____

_____

Day 3:

_____

_____

_____

_____

_____

_____

_____

_____

_____

_____

Day 4:

_____

_____

_____

_____

_____

_____

_____

_____

_____

_____

_____

Day 5:

_____

_____

_____

_____

_____

_____

_____

_____

_____

_____

_____

2. What did your entries teach you this time? Any surprises? Anything you will do differently in the future to help you feel better? Anything you will continue to do because it is working well for you already? Here's a space for your thoughts on this exercise:

_____

_____

_____

_____

_____

_____

_____

_____

_____

_____

_____

SELF-FULL Eating Plan

The keys to SELF-FULL nutrition are balance and moderation.

Balance and Moderation

Eating a meal that is "balanced" assures optimal nutrition and satisfaction. A "balanced" meal is one that has some of each of the following: protein, carbohydrates and fat. Yes, fat. There is a movement afoot these days to banish fat from the American diet. Ironically, since the advent of fat-free food, American have gained an average of eight pounds per person. Part of the reason is that these so-called fat free foods are loaded with calories. Sometimes more than their fat full counterparts. Your body needs fat to function. It needs fat for proper digestion and use of the foods you ingest. A small amount of fat, say a teaspoon of butter or a tablespoon of salad dressing at each meal will go along way to providing your body with the nutrients it needs and the health it so richly deserves.

Eating an imbalanced meal often leads to feelings of hunger and the desire to "graze". When you graze you are mulling around looking for something to eat that will be satisfying. You open and close the refrigerator door. You open and close cabinets and drawers. All in the search for something that will "hit the spot". A balanced meal will usually "hit the spot" and you would not have to go on a "hunt and eat" mission.

Stopping When You Are Full

One of the most SELF-FULL skills you will learn in this process is to stop eating when you are full. The number one reason for obesity is simply eating too much. If you take in more food than your body needs to survive, you will gain weight. There is no magic to this idea. Just fact. To eat enough food to properly nourish your body and at the same time prevent it from gaining weight, you need to stop eating when your body tells you to. And it will. Some people believe that they have no appetite control center in their brain. Much was made of this idea during all the "phen-phen" diet drug publicity. The truth is most people having perfectly functioning appestat centers, they just don't know how to use it.

To use your appetite control center properly you have to listen for it. This is where getting to know yourself and your body will play a vital role. Your body will give off signals when it has had enough food. Just listen. One of the most powerful signals is what I refer to as "the hesitant fork signal." This signal tells you that you have had enough food by causing you to pause ever so slightly as you are bringing food up towards your mouth. There you are popping one French fry into your mouth after another. Then for a split second your rhythm is interrupted. The flow of fries upward from the plate slows ever so subtly. That's the signal. Pay attention for it and you'll notice it. At that moment of hesitation you have a choice. Your body is signaling to you that it has had enough French fries. To eat more would go beyond its nutritional requirements (Yes, French fries have nutritional value. It is when you eat too much of them that their value decreases!) Your choice is between being SELF-FULL and stop eating at this point, knowing that later when you are hungry again you can resume eating, or, to continue eating with the knowledge that this eating is extra and could cause physical problems such as indigestion or excess weight. The choice is yours. Remember that it is easier to hear, understand, and honor your hunger and satiety signals when you know that you can eat again later. Knowing that you will always have access to the foods you love makes this process a snap. Honor your hunger. Respect your fullness and enjoy the pleasure of eating. That is being SELF-FULL.

Other body signals include, a tenderness in the stomach area, a feeling of fatigue or exhaustion, a feeling of nothingness, neither hungry nor full, and an internal sensation of satisfaction. What is your particular body signal?

To get to your "turnoff" point, take a "time-out" during your eating and ask yourself for a status report. Are you still hungry? Are you full? How much more would you like to eat? Listen and you will "hear" the answers.

Exercise. *Feeling Full*

Pay attention to your bodily sensations as you eat. Use the space below to record your observations. Have you identified your "turn-off signal?" If so, what is it? If not, keep listening. Your body will tell you.

_____

_____

_____

_____

_____

_____

_____

_____

_____

Any time you eat beyond hunger, in other words anytime you eat more than your body physically needs, you are eating for emotional reasons. This is an important point. So many people eat for emotional reasons. They eat when they are happy, sad, excited, angry, hurt, frightened, worried, or disappointed. To overcome this source of extra calories you need to address the emotional reasons underlying them. If you can figure out what is making you feel the way you do, you can address the issue directly. When you address the issue directly, you will not have to eat about it. If you do not eat about, you will not gain excess weight. Handling a problem directly is the SELF-FULL way. You will find more information on how to handle problems directly in Chapter Twelve, SELF-FULL Coping Skills. Check it out.

Exercise. *Emotional Eating*

Are you an emotional eater? Here's an exercise to help you identify the emotional reasons why you overeat and what you can do about them.

1. For the next five days record everything you eat or drink in the chart below. Next to each entry record how you were feeling at the time you ate or drank.

| Food/Drink | Feelings |

Day 1

_____

_____

_____

_____

_____

_____

_____

_____

_____

_____

Day 2

_____

_____

_____

_____

_____

_____

_____

_____

_____

_____

Day 3

_____

_____

_____

_____

_____

_____

_____

_____

_____

_____

_____

Day 4

_____

_____

_____

_____

_____

_____

_____

_____

_____

_____

_____

Day 5

_____

_____

_____

_____

_____

_____

_____

_____

_____

_____

_____

_____

2. Review your entries. Do you notice any patterns? Do you tend to eat more in the evening because you are tired? Are Saturdays tough because you are feeling lonely? What patterns are you noticing? Write your insights here.

_____

_____

_____

_____

_____

_____

_____

_____

_____

_____

3. From the patterns that you see emerging, can you think of another way of dealing with your feelings instead of eating? For example, if you tend to overeat at night when you are tired, perhaps going to bed earlier would be a better solution? Or, if you are lonely on Saturdays and are eating because of it, sign up for a Saturday afternoon class instead.

What solutions could you use to deal with your feelings rather than overeat? Put your ideas here.

_____

_____

_____

_____

_____

_____

_____

_____

_____

_____

_____

Food Plan Suggestions

The following plan is a suggestion for how you can improve your daily diet. It goes without saying that if you have any medical conditions that require that you eat or avoid certain foods please make certain you adhere faithfully to your specific needs. To do so is being SELF-FULL.

1. Enjoy fresh fruits and vegetables, lean meats, lean poultry, fish, shellfish, non-fat or low-fat dairy products, whole grains, nuts, seeds, soy, legumes, molasses, honey, oils, and herbal teas.

2. Limit sugars, artificial sweeteners, white flour products, processed or "fake foods", preservatives, additives, excess salt, high fat foods, alcohol, and caffeine.

Sometimes people rely on "filler" foods to help them feel full. Some examples of "filler" foods are diet sodas, popcorn, rice cakes, and celery sticks. The problem with these types of food is that they are rarely satisfying. They may temporarily fill you up but within a short period of time you are searching again for something to eat. It is wiser, translate that to SELF-FULL, to eat that which you are truly hungry for, even if it is a sweet roll, than to fill up of these fillers. In the end you will consume fewer calories if you eat what you truly desire rather than work your way up the food chain from fillers to sweets.

3. Stay hydrated. Drink 6 to 8 glasses of water daily.

4. Take an all natural multi-vitamin that meets the recommended daily allowance. By eating the SELF-FULL way you will not need megadoses of vitamins or minerals.

Remember these are just suggestions. They are here for your information, education, and consideration. Use those that feel right to you. Disregard the rest. Add others that are helpful. You decide what works best for you. The idea is not to be perfect. The idea is to eat a nutritionally sound diet most of the time.

The 3-P's: Planning, Purchasing, and Preparing

To make it easy for you to eat the SELF-FULL way, we will spend some time talking about the 3P's: planning, purchasing, and preparing.

Planning the SELF-FULL Way

Planning your food choices in advance is an excellent way to insure that you will always have SELF-FULL food choices available for you when you want to eat.

An easy way to plan is to create a weekly menu. Figure out what you are likely to eat over the course of a week for breakfast, lunch, dinner and snacks. Use your menu to create a shopping list. Having your pantry stocked with the foods you will eat during the week is an easy way to keep to SELF-FULL eating.

Exercise. *All in a Day's...Food*

Use the space provided to create your first SELF-FULL Menu.

Breakfast   Lunch   Dinner   Snacks

Monday

_____

_____

_____

_____

_____

_____

_____

_____

_____

_____

_____

Tuesday

_____

_____

_____

_____

_____

_____

_____

_____

_____

_____

_____

Wednesday

_____
_____
_____
_____
_____
_____
_____
_____
_____
_____
_____

Thursday

_____
_____
_____
_____
_____
_____
_____
_____
_____
_____
_____

Friday

_____
_____
_____
_____
_____

_____
_____
_____
_____
_____
_____

Saturday
_____
_____
_____
_____
_____
_____
_____
_____
_____
_____
_____

Sunday
_____
_____
_____
_____
_____
_____
_____
_____
_____
_____
_____

To ease your planning, keep a magnetic memo pad on your refrigerator door. Each time you run out of a SELF-FULL food choice jot it down on your memo pad. Then when you are ready to go shopping just pull the list off the pad and you are ready for the market. I recommend a paper pad rather than one of those marker boards so you can take the list with you. If you have to rewrite the list each time before you go shopping chances are you will not always do that and you will end up shopping without a list. Shopping without a list makes it harder to keep your food choices on hand. Keeping your refrigerator stocked with your favorite food choices is an easy way to be SELF-FULL.

Another suggestion is to get yourself one of those insulated lunch bags. I prefer the "six-pack" size, but you choose for yourself what size will best accommodate your needs. Also get a blue ice pack. You should be able to find these items in any large drugstore or supermarket. Fill your lunch bag with the frozen ice pack and your favorite SELF-FULL snacks and carry it with you wherever you go. This way when the need to eat arises you have healthy SELF-FULL food available. It is more SELF-FULL to carry one of these snack packs than it is to dash into a fast food restaurant and gobble down a couple of super size burgers and fries.

Purchasing the SELF-FULL Way

When you are shopping treat yourself to the finest food products you can afford. Choose your favorites not necessarily the bargains. The higher the quality of the food you choose, the more satisfying they are to eat. Why? Because they are generally more flavorful and delicious. The more satisfying the food is the less you will eat. The less you eat the more quickly you will achieve your healthy weight and body size, and stay there! Some people resist buying fresh fruits and vegetables because of the cost. Did you know that pound for pound fresh fruits and vegetables are cheaper than chocolate. A pound of fresh asparagus (one of the most expensive vegetables around) is about $2.99 per pound. A pound of Hershey chocolate (one of the least expensive chocolates around) is about $3.49 a pound. If you do not believe me, check it out for yourself. If you are an ice cream person buy the best. If you like bread, buy fresh from the bakery rather than packages from the shelf. You deserve to feed yourself the best foods the world has to offer. Doing so is another example of being SELF-FULL. Go for it!

Purchasing food and keeping your home filled with your favorites is filling your house with self-care. It is a very SELF-FULL thing to do.

Exercise. *Off to Market!*

Make your first SELF-FULL Shopping List here:

_____
_____
_____
_____
_____
_____
_____
_____
_____
_____
_____

Preparing the SELF-FULL Way

Make life easy for yourself. Buy healthy, fresh foods already prepared. Supermarkets now have fruits and vegetables for sale which are pre-washed and pre-cut. Get those. The deli sections of many finer stores also sell prepared meals, such as chicken and poached salmon. Check out the stores in your neighborhood. See what they are offering that is healthy and ready made. I think you will be delighted with what is now available. They may cost a bit more, but you are definitely worth it. If you need to rationalize spending the money, think of all the money you will save because you will feel better (no extra doctor visits), or because you will stay at a healthy weight (no more buying new clothes because the old ones are too small), shall I go on?

If you are not so lucky as to have these types of items available for you, you can still makes things easier for yourself with a little bit of effort up front. Here are some ideas:

1. When you get home from the supermarket, immediately wash your fruits and vegetables. Those that need cutting up, cut up, store in clear plastic bags or containers for easy access during the week.

2. Divide your meat and fish purchase into portions and freeze or refrigerate individually.

3. When you are cooking or baking, double your recipes and freeze individual portion sizes for later use. Get a freezer pen and mark on the outside of the package what it contains and the date you froze it. Use older items first.

With regard to actual food preparation, here are some tips to help you eat the SELF-FULL way:

1. Use chicken or vegetable broth when cooking in place of butter or margarine. Try it in mashed potatoes, it's delicious.

2. Use unsweetened applesauce in place of oil when baking.

3. Toss in dried fruit, such as raisins or apricots into muffin recipes for extra nutrition.

4. Make your salads huge. Toss in every vegetable you like. Add some beans for crunch and some low-fat cheese for calcium and protein.

5. Use salsa in place of sour cream on baked potatoes and in meat-loaf in place of oil.

These are just a few suggestions. Can you think of any on your own? Put your suggestions here:

_____

_____

_____

_____

_____

_____

_____

_____

_____

_____

_____

_____

Peaceful Eating

SELF-FULL eating is peaceful eating. It means taking a "time out" to nourish yourself and rejuvenate. We all know that eating on the run leads to poor food choices, overeating, indigestion, fatigue, and cravings. I find that it is better to take 15 minutes to sit quietly, without distractions (except maybe soft, soothing music), and eat, than to eat distractedly on the run. For one thing, the food tastes better. For another, you will tend to eat less and make healthier choices.

Where are you on the subject of peaceful eating? Here's an exercise to help you find out.

Exercise. Band on the Run

1. Do you tend to eat on the run? When? Which meals?

_____

_____

_____

_____

_____
_____
_____
_____
_____
_____
_____
_____

2 What are your reasons for not taking the time to eat peacefully?

_____
_____
_____
_____
_____
_____
_____
_____
_____
_____
_____

3. Do your reasons still make sense to you?

_____
_____
_____
_____
_____
_____
_____
_____

_____

_____

4. Would you like to change? If so, how can you start to eat more peacefully?

_____

_____

_____

_____

_____

_____

_____

_____

_____

_____

_____

In the Company of Others

SELF-FULLNESS is about being able to take care of yourself in the presence of others. This includes meal time. For many of us, meals are emotionally charged times in our lives. It may be the only time the entire family is together. It may be a lonely time, when you wish you had a family to share a meal with. It maybe a time when issues get discussed or feelings get pushed "under the table." When meal times are for other purposes besides nourishment, being SELF-FULL becomes extremely important.

Exercise. Meal time Memories

1. Take a moment to reflect on your meal time memories, past and present. Do meal times present a dilemma in your quest to be SELF-FULL? If so, how?

_____

_____

_____

_____

_____

_____

_____

_____

_____

_____

_____

2. Who interferes and how? Is it your father telling to finish everything on your plate because children are starving in other parts of the world? Or, is your husband complaining about how much money you spend? Or, is the problem your mother-in-law who can't cook to save her life and yet you feel obliged to eat her concoctions anyway?

_____

_____

_____

_____

_____

_____

_____

_____

_____

_____

_____

3. What would a SELF-FULL action be for you in your situation? Leaving food over when you are no longer hungry? Saying "thanks, but no thanks" to your mother-in-law?

_____

_____

_____

_____

_____

_____

_____

_____

_____

_____

_____

_____

4. What would happen if you acted in a SELF-FULL way? How would you feel? Who would be helped? Who would be hurt?

_____

_____

_____

_____

_____

_____

_____

_____

_____

_____

_____

5. Can you think of a creative solution to your particular problem? A solution where you can be SELF-FULL and at the same time spare another's feelings? How about donating some money to UNICEF instead of eating the extra food in your plate? How about putting less food on your plate to begin with? Or, how about taking home some of

your mother-in law's food for the dog or the trash? What could work for you?

_____

_____

_____

_____

_____

_____

_____

_____

_____

_____

There may be some people with whom sharing a meal is no longer in your best interest. If being with someone at a meal is too upsetting for whatever reason, choose to spend time with that person in other ways. Spending time with that person in another setting is an appropriate SELF-FULL response.

Here's an example from one of my patients. Her name is Sylvia. Sylvia is currently very overweight. She is working hard in her therapy to understand why she overeats and is trying to make better choices. Sylvia's sister, Connie, is slim. Sylvia and Connie have lunch once a week. The problem is whenever Sylvia eats with Connie, Connie constantly scrutinizes everything Sylvia eats. Poor Sylvia can't get a bite of food into her mouth without Connie making a comment. As a consequence, meals with Connie are very stressful for Sylvia. She finds herself picking at her food in Connie's presence and then bingeing on food when she gets home. Obviously it is not in Sylvia's best interest to continue seeing Connie for lunch. Because having a relationship with her sister is important to Sylvia, I suggested that she and Connie meet for weekly manicures instead of weekly lunches. Sylvia tried it and found that she was much more relaxed around Connie, could enjoy her sister more, and after they parted company no longer felt like she need to eat half of LA County. Plus her hands never looked prettier.

6. Following Sylvia's lead, who do you need to see outside a "food setting?" What alternative plan can you come up with?

_____

_____

_____

_____

_____

_____

_____

_____

_____

_____

_____

A Word about Eating Disorders

Much of my private practice experience has been in the treatment of eating disorders, particularly anorexia and bulimia. Simply put, a person who is anorexic is severely underweight and a person with bulimia will overeat large quantities of food and then use various methods to get rid of the food, such as vomiting, using laxative, or over exercising. If you or someone you know has such a disorder, I urge you to seek appropriate help immediately. These disorders can be life threatening. They can also be successfully treated. For more information on these disorders, contact your physician or a mental health practitioner who specializes in the treatment of eating disorders. For more on how to find a qualified mental health professional, see Chapter Five on SELF-FULL Health.

3

SELF-FULL FITNESS

SELF-FULL Fitness is not about getting into swimsuit shape. It is about learning to love and respect your body. It is about recognizing your body's wonders, its abilities and functions, its beauty and role in your life.

Exercise. Body Appreciation

This exercise is called body appreciation. Its intention is to get you to appreciate the splendor of your body. Have you ever really thought about your body and all the things it does for you on any given day? Let's take a moment to do so.

1. Here is a list of some of your body parts. Make a note next to each one indicating what it does for you or how it helps you get through your day:

Eyes _____

Nose _____

Ears_____

Upper Arms _____

Wrists _____

Hands_____

Shoulders _____

Stomach _____

Thighs_____

Calves _____

Feet_____

What did you notice as you did this exercise? Did you notice how important even the smallest part of your body is? Does this insight make you want to take better care of your body? Why or why not? Record your revelations here:

_____
_____
_____
_____
_____
_____
_____
_____
_____

_____
_____

2. Everyday, pay attention to your body. Appreciate it for its intricacies and wonders. Thank it for its help in your life. For example, when you are in the shower, acknowledge each part of your body as you wash it. Or, as you sit or drive your car be grateful for the parts of your body that are participating in those endeavors. After you have done this for a while, write down your thoughts about your body here:

_____
_____
_____
_____
_____
_____
_____
_____
_____
_____
_____

Let's Get Physical

Moderate and consistent exercise is important to SELF-FULL living. Such exercise will reduce anxiety, depression, and stress. It will also increase the restfulness of your sleep, improve your ability to cope with life dilemmas, and enhance the clarity of your thinking.

There are many exercises to choose from. You can pick aerobic exercises like swimming, running, walking, hiking, roller blading, or ice skating. Or, if your prefer, you can choose from the recreational sports such as tennis, golf, basketball, skiing, or softball. There are also anaerobic forms of fitness. These include yoga, weight-lifting, stretching, and toning.

There's No Right Way—Only Your Way

There are so many books and magazines devoted to exercise. Each "allegedly" offering *the* answer to your exercise woes. The problem is these books and magazines often offer a different solution.

So what are you to do? Do the SELF-FULL thing and listen to yourself. The "best" exercise for you is the exercise you will do! It is as easy as that. For some people, their exercise of choice is running. For others it is golf or tennis. It does not matter which exercise you choose. What is important is that whatever exercise you choose you do consistently.

To help you along in figuring out which fitness activity will work for you, try the following exercise.

Exercise. What fitness activities do you enjoy?

1. Make a list of all the fitness activities that you have tried over your lifetime. Think back to grammar school and high school for starters.

_____

_____

_____

_____

_____

_____

_____

_____

_____

2. Once you have your list, re-order the list by level of enjoyment. Put the activities you enjoyed participating in on the top of your list and the ones you did not enjoy on the bottom.

_____
_____
_____
_____
_____
_____
_____
_____
_____
_____
_____

3. Now, take a look at your list. Are there any activities on your list that you still participate in? If so, those activities may be good places to start your SELF-FULLNESS fitness plan. Why? Because they are the activities that you seem to be continuing over your life span.

_____
_____
_____
_____
_____
_____
_____
_____
_____
_____
_____

4. Next, continuing to look at your list, are there any activities that you would like to participate in again? For example, let us say you played volleyball in high school and you remember it being a lot of fun. Why not join a team and start playing again? Check out your local adult

education class schedules and the local park and recreations departments for ideas. You will be surprised how much is available for adults. List the activities that you might want to give a whirl.

_____

_____

_____

_____

_____

_____

_____

_____

_____

_____

_____

To keep exercise fun, choose an activity you enjoy. Engage in a variety of activities to prevent injury, burn-out and boredom. If you exercise at home you can make it fun by watching your favorite television program, reading your favorite magazine or book or listening to great music. There are tapes you can buy that are specifically designed for work-outs. Check your local sporting goods store for ideas.

Exercise. *What makes fitness fun for you?*

1. What makes exercise fun for you? Tapes? A companion? A personal trainer? A TV? A radio? Make a list of the ways that you can make exercise fun for you.

_____

_____

_____

_____

_____

_____
_____
_____
_____
_____

2. What activities can you add to your fitness routine so that you stay enthusiastic and motivated to continue?

_____
_____
_____
_____
_____
_____
_____
_____
_____
_____
_____

Your SELF-FULL Fitness Plan

Here's a way to design your own SELF-FULL Fitness plan. Remember to keep your focus on how the exercise feels and how it is helping you take care of yourself.

Get it in Writing

An important key for fitness success is keeping a record of your activities. You can use any blank book or notebook. Make the log continuous. The reason for doing this is to keep you going. If you keep your log a week at a time and miss a day you may be inclined to skip the rest of the week and just "start again on Monday". A continuous log can prevent that.

Keeping up and Keep on Going

Once you are started on an exercise routine, you need to find ways to keep it alive. Gyms count on the fact that people sign up for their services and then quit shortly thereafter. This allows the gyms to continue to invite new members to join without worrying that the gym will become too crowded.

For you to stay in gear, focus in how exercise makes you feel. Reframe your use of exercise from weight loss or management to how it feels, both physically and emotionally. You may find after a little while that you are less winded walking up the stairs to your apartment. You may also find that you are sleeping better and feeling well rested. You may also notice that you suffer from the "blues" far less often after you have established your fitness routine.

Keep track of how you feel as a result of your fitness routine in your exercise log. Use your entries to keep you motivated to keep on keeping on!

Another way to make exercise a permanent part of your life is to follow your SELF-FULL fitness plan for a minimum of six months. After six months, the "habit" of exercise should be well ingrained in your lifestyle and a normal part of your daily and weekly routine.

Here are some suggestions on how to make exercise a valued part of your life:

1. Make an appointment with yourself to exercise. Write it in your date book as you would any other appointment. Your appointment with yourself is as valuable as your appointment with the vet or car mechanic.

2. If you travel, plan to walk around the airport during lay-overs or around the city you are visiting. Take along a jump rope. Stay in a hotel that has a gym or swimming pool.

Exercise. Staying Motivated

What can you do to stay motivated? Put your plan of action here.

_____
_____
_____
_____
_____
_____
_____
_____
_____
_____
_____

STOP! if it Hurts

The old adage *"no pain, no gain"* is not a SELF-FULL notion. Common sense tells you that if something hurts, stop doing it. This is especially true in the area of physical fitness.

If stopping your exercise when you feel pain is not enough to provide relief, have your ailment checked out by a doctor. Stop also if you feel breathless, dizzy, or faint. There is nothing SELF-FULL about passing out on the gym floor!

More SELF-FULLNESS to come...

Let's take a break from our focus in your physical well-being and move along to your interpersonal relationships. The next chapter takes a look at improving your relationships at home, at work, and at play. We will return to your physical well-being again in Chapter Five when we explore SELF-FULL Health.

4

SELF-FULL RELATIONSHIPS

Being SELF-FULL with Others

In the Chapter on SELF-FULL Eating, I raised the notion that sometimes you must be willing to end a relationship that is not working or is hurting you. In this chapter, we will explore ways to make your relationships more satisfying and fulfilling. We will also look at when it becomes necessary to end a relationship to protect yourself from harm.

Let's take a look at the skills you can develop to help you in your relationships.

Interpersonal Skills

The interpersonal skills you will be learning are acknowledging others, boundary setting, assertiveness, and listening

Acknowledging Good in Others

Positive feelings are the grease that keep the wheels of a relationship, any relationship, moving smoothly. Learning how to make another person feel good about themselves and about you is a key ingredient in forming long-lasting loving, nurturing relationships. I am not talking about false compliments or two-faced hypocrisy. I am talking about genuine positive feeling exchanged between two or more people.

One way to accomplish this is to look for the best in the people you meet. Everyone has something to offer. One person may be very dependable. Another a good listener. Someone else may be fun to go to a concert with. Pay close attention to the people you share your life with. Notice what each "brings to the table." When you see the good in a person let them know it. Tell your friend who is a good listener how much you appreciate her time. Let your fun friend know that you truly enjoy her company. You don't have to be gushy or sentimental about it. Merely state it or write a short note of thanks. Doing this will make the person receiving your acknowledgment feel good. People like to spend time with people who make them feel good.

Exercise. Pleasing People

Here's a simple exercise to get you thinking about the people in your life and what is good about them.

1. Who are some of the people in your life? List their names here.

_____

_____

_____

_____

_____

_____

_____

_____

_____

_____

_____

2. Can you think of something positive about them that they bring into your life? For each person you identified in 1, list a positive attribute or two.

_____

_____

_____

_____

_____

_____

_____

_____

_____

_____

_____

3. Have you told them what you like about them? Could you? How? When? Make a note for each person identified of what, how, and when you will acknowledge what you like about them.

_____

_____

_____

_____

_____

_____

_____

_____

_____

Acknowledging Other's Feelings

Acknowledging others also includes acknowledging that others have feelings, too! It is very important for you to understand that someone may have a different response or reaction to a situation than you do. Just as you are striving to be recognized and understood for who you are, you must do the same for others if you want to have healthy interpersonal relationships.

Everyone is entitled to their feelings. There is no right or wrong way to feel in any given situation. It is important to let others have their reactions. They, like you, need to feel acknowledged and validated. Practice acknowledging the feelings of others, by saying something along the lines of "I can understand why you feel that way. I, however, feel differently." Or, "I understand that you are upset right now and I am sorry about that". Trying to get someone else to change their feelings is nearly impossible and certainly not worth the effort. As you practice accepting and acknowledging other's feelings, you will be more able to accept your own feelings and others will be more receptive to accepting yours too.

Setting Boundaries

One of the most important skills you will learn in your pursuit of SELF-FULLNESS is setting boundaries. Setting boundaries is the SELF-FULL way to establish the parameters of a relationship. It is the way to teach someone how to treat you. It is a statement to others of how you would like to spend your time and your energy. It states how much privacy and emotional space you need.

Setting limits gently and effectively is an excellent way to set boundaries. Setting limits means saying no to the demands of others when these demands go against your best interest. Common areas of limit setting include time, money, and privacy. If you do not set limits you may find yourself resenting the other person. In time you and that other person may grow apart. A friendship that may have had potential is lost.

Here's a common example to illustrate the importance of setting appropriate boundaries. Many women make a mistake when they are dating. They allow the man to make all the decisions about when they will see each other, where, for how long and so on. They do this thinking that the man should be the initiator, the aggressor. They are afraid that if they say what they want or initiate contact or a plan, they will seem pushy and undesirable. Many women place themselves in a passive role in the relationship and they complain about it later. They allow the man to "be in control" from the beginning and then later resent him for being "controlling." The problem with this approach is that the woman teaches the man that it is okay to have this form of a relationship. Later when the women wants to participate more the man gets angry, upset or confused. All of a sudden she is "changing the rules" and the trouble begins. If from the start the woman had shown her true desires, one of two things would have happened. Either it would have been discovered early on that the couple is incompatible which would have saved a lot of heartache and pain later, or, the balance of power in the relationship would have been established from the beginning and it would have been smoother sailing in the long run.

Drawing Firm, Clear Boundaries

Many people are afraid to set these boundaries because of fear. They are afraid that they won't be liked. They are afraid others will leave them or will get angry with them. To effectively set boundaries, you need to understand your rights in any situation and appreciate your entitlement to those rights. You must learn to refuse to be treated in a harsh or unfair manner.

To set limits you must do so clearly. To find out what your limits are ask yourself what you need in this particular situation. Limit setting is not an all or nothing situation. To set limits start with a polite statement of your needs. Often that is enough. If that is ineffective, raise the tone of your voice and the words you choose. If that does not get the result you desire, add a consequence. If that does not work, follow through on the consequence. One consequence may be walking away from the situation. This is not the same thing as giving in. Leaving a negative situation can be a very SELF-FULL thing to do.

Stop Reinforcing Negative Behavior

Another way to set boundaries is by not reinforcing negative behaviors. For example, let's say someone keeps coming late to a meeting. Instead of addressing the tardiness, you ignore it by bringing the late comer up to date and reviewing everything that happened before he entered. Doing so reinforces the tardiness. It is unspoken permission to continue be late because there are no consequences to the latecomer. However, if you did not bring him up to date he would feel the consequences of his tardiness and come on time the next time. You have just set a boundary with respect to your time without having to address it directly. This is a very effective way to set boundaries.

Initiating Boundaries

Lastly, it is important to initiate boundaries instead of reacting to intrusions. This is actually more comfortable and usually gets better results.

Exercise. A Line in the Sand

Let's get some practice with boundary setting.

1. Think of a situation you are currently in where your boundaries are being intruded upon. Is it at work? At home?

_____

_____

_____

_____

_____

_____

_____

_____

_____

_____

2. What boundary do you need to set to feel comfortable in that situation?

_____

_____

_____

_____

_____

_____

_____

_____

_____

_____

3. Write down a description of exactly what you would like to do or say
to set the boundary.

_____
_____
_____
_____
_____
_____
_____
_____
_____
_____
_____
_____

4. Practice saying or doing that very thing with someone trustworthy
(like a close friend or therapist) until it feels comfortable. Then move
on to the real situation and go for it! You'll feel wonderful afterward.

Assertiveness Training

The next area we will address in the realm of SELF-FULL
Relationships is assertiveness. Interestingly, we all arrive in the world
fully equipped to assert ourselves. But our families, churches, schools,
and culture serve to shut down this valuable skill. We are born with as
much right to have opinions and feelings as anyone else but we do not
act that way. Learning to assert yourself is single-handily the most effective way to act SELF-FULL. By taking the risk and identifying your
needs and wants and acting on your own behalf you can create the life
you want.

It is important to note that by being assertive you do not guarantee
that you will get everything you ask for. The power comes in the asking
not necessarily in the receiving.

What is Assertiveness?

Assertiveness is the ability to state your feelings, opinions, needs, wants, and desires without fear, anxiety or embarrassment. It is allowing yourself to be taken into account while at the same time taking into account the feelings, opinions, and needs of others. It means getting in touch with your feelings and your power. Yes, power. You are a powerful individual. You may just not know it yet.

By being assertive you are protecting yourself from others' intrusions and aggressions. Failing to act assertively usually leads to emotional distress, very often in the form of depression.

Acting assertively is different than acting aggressively. Acting aggressively is being the bully. Acting assertively is being the confident self-assured woman that you are. Assertion is not aggression.

I would like to offer a brief word about anxiety. Often when a person begins to practice assertiveness, he or she experiences anxiety. If that happens to you, please do not be frightened. Please do not use this a reason to abandon your quest to be assertive. This is a natural response to a new, unfamiliar situation. Over time, as you practice your assertiveness skills in different situations and achieve positive results from doing so, your anxiety will fade. You will become more relaxed as a result of your new found skills and eventually your anxiety will disappear.

Being Assertive Means Being Direct

Being assertive means being direct-saying exactly what you think or feel. Being direct in your communication cuts down on the chance that you will be misunderstood by your listener. Sometimes misunderstandings happen accidentally. You think you said what you intended to convey, but it is received differently. Sending the clearest possible message is the antidote for potential misunderstandings. To send a clear message keep it void of innuendoes, subtleties or nuances. Make your message complete. Avoid giving only a limited picture of the subject you are speaking about. Include all relevant details.

Being Assertive Means Not Having to Apologize for Who You Are

Stop apologizing for yourself and who you are. Stop explaining your reasons for why you are doing what you are doing. You do not owe anyone any explanations.

Being Assertive Means Being Honest

Being assertive also means being honest. By being honest you say what you really feel. Not what you should feel or what someone else tells you to feel. You state your feelings separate from any value judgments.

Being Assertive Means Being Timely

Being assertive also means speaking your feelings as soon as possible. By speaking directly, honestly, and promptly you protect yourself from misunderstandings and hurt feelings. Your feelings will be expressed one way or another. They have to. That is the nature of feelings. If you are unable to express your feeling assertively they will show themselves some other way. Take the lesson from Sarah and her roommate Leslie. Sarah was angry at Leslie for leaving dirty dishes in the sink overnight in violation of their house rules. If Sarah had acted assertively she would have acknowledged her feelings directly and honestly to Leslie first thing in the morning. Instead, Sarah stewed. She did not say anything and got more and more angry with Leslie as the week went along. Her resentment towards Leslie was really building. Eventually Sarah "acted out" her anger at Leslie indirectly by not telling her about an important phone call she received. When Leslie learned of the phone call she was also angry. Irreparable damage resulted between the two and they soon parted company. This damage could have been avoided if Sarah had spoken her angry feelings to Leslie assertively.

Assertive Body Language

Direct eye contact tells the listener that you mean what you say. Avoiding shifting your eyes away as you make your important point. Maintain eye contact for a few seconds after you have said what you have needed to say.

Tone of voice is important too. A high pitch squeaky sound does not reflect confidence and assurance. Nor does a childlike little voice. Use a firm tone. Increase your volume without being unnecessarily loud. Practice with a tape recorder or with a trusted friend to get it right.

Good posture also reflects confidence and tells the listener that you are sure of your position. It gives you credibility. So listen to what your grandmother always told you and stand up straight!

The Power of "I"

The most effective way to express your assertion is through the use of "I" statements. An example of an "I" statement is "I feel angry when you walk out of the room when I am speaking." A "you" statement such as "You really make me mad when you walk out of the room when I am speaking" is much less effective. Using "you" statements is aggressive and can leave the listener defensive, feeling under attack, and unwilling to hear what you have to say. Let's practice for a moment with "I" statement before we move on.

Exercise. The Power of I

1. Change the following "You" statements into "I" statements:

"You make me so mad when you call me lazy."

_____
_____
_____

"You are so mean to me sometimes."

_____
_____
_____

"You are really inconsiderate by not coming home on time."

_____
_____
_____

"You don't understand me."

_____
_____
_____

"You always put me down."

_____
_____
_____

2. Would you rather be on the receiving end of an "I" statement or a "You" statement? Why?

_____
_____
_____
_____
_____

_____
_____
_____
_____
_____
_____

3. Is there an "I" statement you need to make? Write it down here.

_____
_____
_____
_____
_____
_____
_____
_____
_____
_____

4. Practice your "I" statement for a while either alone or with a friend and then, when you are ready, say it to the person who needs to hear it. Record your experience here. Good luck!

_____
_____
_____
_____
_____
_____
_____
_____
_____

Deal With Feelings

In a previous discussion we accepted the notion that good interpersonal relationships include an acknowledgment of other's feelings. When you are in a difficult or confrontational situation it is helpful to step away from the surface problem to the feelings underneath. Remember that everyone has a right to his or her feelings and everyone has the right to have different ones about the same situation. In these moments it is instructive to agree to disagree. Sometime focusing on a person's intention rather than on the words they said or the actions they took can also help.

Here's an example that illustrates this point. Claudia, a 38 year old account executive at an ad agency, was upset one day because she was wrongfully reprimanded by her boss. She called her mother to get some comfort and instead she got dismissed. In response to Claudia's feelings, her mother said "Claudia, don't feel that way. Your boss was just doing her job. Get over it. You can't afford to lose your job." Claudia felt anger in response to her mother's comments. I encouraged Claudia to look beyond her mother's words to her intention. It seemed to me that Claudia's mother was uncomfortable with Claudia's sadness. She was also worried about Claudia's financial situation. What her mother intended was for Claudia to be safe, to keep her job. Once Claudia could understand her mother's intent she was less angry and could reply to her mother in an assertive way. She said " Mom, I know you meant well when you told me not to feel bad about my boss. I understand that you were only concerned for my welfare. However, in the future it would help me if you just hear me out and allow me to have my feelings without offering your suggestions. I would find that particularly helpful."

Back up Your Assertive Statements with Action

Sometimes it becomes necessary to back up your assertions with action. I am not talking about idle threats, they are meaningless. No, I am talking about actions you are willing to live with. A little of bit of "muscle" so to speak.

Let's take Claudia as an example again. Let's say she made her assertive statement to her mother and her mother did not comply. Instead she kept on offering unwelcome suggestions. An action Claudia could take would be to end the telephone call. She could say "Mom, if you continue to speak with me this way, I will need to end this conversation." If her mother continues, Claudia's next best action would be to end the conversation by telling her mother that their conversation cannot continue and then hanging up the phone. If Claudia said she would hang up the phone and didn't she would lose credibility so that the next time she attempts to assert herself with her mother she would have less leverage. That's why it is important for you to choose actions that you can follow through with. When you do, it is very powerful and effective.

Accepting Criticism

The last arena of assertiveness training we will tackle is the dealing with criticism. The trick to taking the bite out a critical remark is to respond to the remark without apology, in a non-attacking, non-defensive manner. When faced with criticism, your choices are to accept the criticism, disagree with it, set limits with the person who made the remark, delay making a response, or merely acknowledge it without disagreement or agreement.

It may happen that the criticism you receive is valid. The person is correctly point out to you something that is worthwhile for you to consider. If this is the case, your most assertive response is to simple accept the criticism and if you are so inclined to thank the person offering it.

If you disagree with the criticism then state your disagreement and then follow with a self-affirming statement.

To set limits with respect to criticism, teach the person how to give you negative feedback. Teach the person how you prefer to be spoken to in these matters.

If you are uncertain how to respond simply buy yourself some time by stating your need to think about the comment. This allows you to gather your thoughts and feelings rather than react in the heat of the moment.

Lastly, you can also simply acknowledge the criticism without agreeing or disagreeing.

Before we move on to the next interpersonal skill, listening, here's an exercise to help you hone your assertiveness.

Exercise. *Assertiveness Training 101*

1. Pick a situation in your life where you need to be assertive. Describe it here.

_____

_____

_____

_____

_____

_____

_____

_____

_____

_____

_____

2. Use the space below to "script" the conversation you need to have.

_____

_____

_____
_____
_____
_____
_____
_____
_____
_____
_____
_____

3. If your conversation is ineffective, what action would you be willing to do to get your point across?

_____
_____
_____
_____
_____
_____
_____
_____
_____
_____
_____

Listening Skills

There are three element of good listening. They are (1) direct eye contact; (2) acknowledging the speaker; and, (3) listening actively.

Direct eye contact tells the speaker that they have your attention. Practice looking into people's eye when they speak . If that is too hard, looking at their forehead gives the appearance that you are looking directly at them.

When someone is speaking to you it is foremost important to acknowledge their message. Simple tell them that you heard and understood what they said. You do not need to agree or disagree. Good listening involves merely acknowledging receipt of the message. Many hurt feelings can be avoided by a simple acknowledgment of a communication.

Active listening is trying to understand the meaning of the message being sent, not just hearing the words. When you hear the message, repeat back to the sender, in your own words, what you understood the message to mean. You do not agree or disagree you merely reflect the intention and meaning of the message as you understood it. This gives the sender an opportunity to restate the message if it is not being correctly understood.

Exercise. Active Listening 101

Practice your listening skills with everyone you meet. With time you will become better and better at it. Record your experiences here.

_____

_____

_____

_____

_____

_____

_____

_____

_____

_____

_____

_____

_____

_____

SELF-FULLNESS at Home

The communication skills we have been looking at are as effective in the living room as they are in the boardroom. Applying what you learned above to situations at home can take your family life to a wonderful new level. Just remember that effective communication involves both the sending of information and the receiving of it. To be effectively understood, you need to make certain that the intention of your message is clearly stated, that it is directly communicated to the listener and that it is received by the listener. A failure at any of these levels can lead to misunderstanding and subsequently conflict.

It is especially important in personal relationships to speak from the "I" rather than "you" position. Remember saying "I want" or "I need" is much more effective than saying "you did". It also helps if the intensity of your message is also clear. For example, if you are enthusiastic about something let that show. If something is very important to you say so. Do not assume that the other person knows how important or unimportant something is to you. You owe it to yourself and to your listener to be as clear as possible. Remember to be direct, honest, timely and use appropriate "muscle".

SELF-FULL Marriage

A SELF-FULL marriage has a "her" part, a "his" part and an "our" part. To be SELF-FULL in a marriage is to allow yourself be a separate entity within the marriage. Asking for and claiming personal space and autonomy is healthy and necessary for a successful marriage.

A person who sees herself as complete in her own right is better able to have a healthy, SELF-FULL marriage. This allows the most successful marriage to take place—a marriage between equals.

From the beginning educate your spouse on how you want to be treated. Recall our discussion on setting boundaries in Chapter Four. In that discussion, I gave an example of what some women do at the beginning of a relationship. They defer to the man's wishes and later get angry when they don't get their needs met. I call this the "old bait and switch." I hear about it all the time. Because the woman was "dishonest" with herself and her husband in the beginning of the relationship a lot of problems erupt later. The best way to prevent this from happening is to know yourself and express yourself from the beginning. To do otherwise creates a "fantasy marriage". Allowing a fantasy marriage to occur hurts everyone.

SELF-FULL Parenting

Effective parenting begins with effective living. You teach your children how to be in the world more by what you do than what you say. If you tell your children that smoking is dangerous for their heath and then light up yourself it should come as no surprise to learn later that your kids are smoking. If you are overweight because you cope with your problems by overeating, your children may develop the same habit. By adopting the principles, concepts and skills of SELF-FULL-NESS and applying them to your daily life you will set a healthy example for your children to emulate.

SELF-FULL Families

There is an old expression "a family who prays together stays together." Make SELF-FULLNESS a way of life in your family and you too will "stay together!"

SELF-FULLNESS at Work

Dealing with supervisors, subordinates, and peers can be challenging in even the most pleasant of work environments. Depending on how big your company is, you may be dealing with tens if not hundreds of different personalities.

SELF-FULLNESS at work occurs when you are able to maintain a professional disposition, are respected by your co-workers and subordinates, and appreciated by your superiors.

In dealing with people on the job it is important to combine strength with sensitivity. Being too nice is ineffective and diminishes the respect you get from others. Coming on too strong gets short-term cooperation but long-term resistance. Learn to treat others with openness and respect. Always listen attentively.

To improve your relationships at work, try to figure out what you can do that will add value to your relationships. Ask your boss or co-worker what would help them. When you add value to another person's life you become valued.

A danger that many working women suffer from is being too nurturing on the job. Women who make it a habit of taking care of others often find themselves at the mercy of demanding and often times unscrupulous bosses and co-workers. A woman who habitually performs these nurturing functions, such as always getting coffee for her peers or staying late to cover the phones when someone asks her, can compromise her professional standing and credibility. This does not mean that you are not to be a "team player." It means that you avoid the rescue role at work.

Perhaps you are in a position of authority. How do you exercise authority in a SELF-FULL manner?

To exert authority make certain that your verbal and non-verbal messages are congruent. In other words, make certain your words and your actions are consistent. That they "say" the same thing. In addition, keep to your agenda. Doing so also reflects consistency which is a necessary ingredient to maintaining authority.

Lastly, in dealing with people at work it is SELF-FULL to present yourself in a positive manner. Put your best foot forward and you will travel far.

Here's an exercise to get you on your way.

Exercise. *Putting Your Best Foot Forward*

1. Make a list of your accomplishments. They can be anything from getting a high school diploma to having a baby.

_____

_____

_____

_____

_____

_____

_____

_____

_____

_____

2. Now, make a list of your positive qualities, such as promptness, kindness, good sense of humor.

_____

_____

_____

_____

_____

_____

_____

_____

_____

3. Now turn your positive qualities into affirmations. Such as "I am a kind and giving person."

_____

_____

_____

_____

_____

_____

_____

_____

_____

_____

4. Repeat these affirmations to yourself daily. Write them on a sheet of paper and carry them with you in your briefcase or daily planner. When you start to feel unsure of yourself, pull them out for a quick refresher course on who you are and what you are capable of. It will do wonders for your self-image and your job performance. Where did you put your affirmations?

_____

_____

_____

_____

_____

_____

_____

_____

_____

_____

In Your Community

Are you an active member of your community? Do you know your neighbors? In a society that is becoming as isolative as ours, the importance of community cannot be overstated. A community can be your neighborhood, or your church or synagogue. It can be a chorus you sing in or a board you serve on.

A SELF-FULL life is a well-rounded life so that includes having a community to belong to. What is your community? If you don't have one, you can find one.

Exercise. A Sense of Belonging

1. If you find yourself without a community or a sense of belonging, you can create it for yourself. One way is to think about with whom you would like to spend time. With whom you would like to share your life. In the space provided, list the people or organizations that you would like to be a part of if you could.

_____

_____

_____

_____

_____

_____

_____

_____

_____

_____

_____

2. Where do these people or groups congregate?

_____

_____

_____

_____

_____

_____

_____

_____

_____

_____

_____

3. Make plans to connect with these people the next time they have an event or meeting. Or, invite someone you would like to know to an event of your own and start the ball rolling. What will you do?

_____

_____

_____

_____

_____

_____

_____

_____

_____

_____

_____

About Intimacy

Have you noticed that everyone is talking about intimacy? More specifically, intimacy "problems?" Turn on any talk show and someone is complaining about someone else's intimacy problem. Intimacy is sadly misunderstood. Intimacy is often confused for sex. Of course, there is sexual intimacy. That's the kind of intimacy that two people share when they make love. Emotional intimacy is something else. Emotional intimacy is the ability for people to be themselves in the presence of others. When you are intimate you are able to be who you are with all your "imperfections" and "flaws". You are not hiding behind some pretense or lie. You are open and available. In an intimate relationship you allow yourself to be vulnerable.

If you find yourself in a relationship with someone who has "intimacy problems", take a good hard look at yourself. Are you able to be open and free in the presence of another or do you hide parts of yourself? In psychology circles we often talk about the person with whom you have a relationship as a "mirror" of yourself. They "reflect" back to you the very "issues" you are struggling with.

To have a successful intimate relationship you have to be willing to be intimate yourself. To be intimate with another you need to know and understand yourself. Fortunately for you you are doing just that as you become more SELF-FULL.

SELF-FULL Dating

In your quest for a SELF-FULL intimate relationship you will do a lot of dating. At least I hope you will do A LOT of dating. Why? Because dating is about meeting a lot of people so you can find out who YOU are in a relationship and who you would be compatible with for the long run. Too many people stop dating others as soon as they meet someone who wants to date them! Is this you? Until you are in a committed relationship that looks and feels right to you, I encourage you to keep on dating.

If you find dating hard, think of it as a vehicle for your personal growth. Pay attention to who you are on a date. Notice whether you are out-going and talkative or passive and quiet. Does your demeanor change depending on whom you are dating? Do certain people bring out the best in you? Do others bring out your worst? In whose company are you comfortable? Who makes you nervous? The more you learn about yourself the better choice you will make in a mate.

Also spend your dating time getting to know the person you are seeing. People tend to "project" who they want the person to be rather than really getting to know who they are. Spend time getting to know someone. Learn his moods. Learn her likes and dislikes. It is easier to do this if you are also dating others. You won't be so "desperate" for this one to be "the one." And for heaven's sake don't jump into bed after the first date. Be SELF-FULL. Take care of yourself. Protect your body as well as your heart.

About Sex

Since we are on the subject of sex, let's take another look at it. A physically and emotionally healthy person has needs. That's a fact. To act on those needs is not "bad" or "dirty". (Unless, of course, doing so contradicts your religious convictions in which case, the SELF-FULL way is to honor your convictions and be proud of your commitment to yourself.)

What is harmful is having sex too soon with someone you hardly know and having unprotected sex. In the next Chapter on SELF-FULL Health, we will take an uncensored look at the consequences of unprotected sex, but for now, keep in mind that you have only one heart and one body, protect both of them. Insist on condoms and blood tests. I know it is awkward in the heat of passion to talk about these things so TALK ABOUT THEM FIRST. If you cannot have a conversation with the person you are about to sleep with about these subjects YOU HAVE NO BUSINESS SLEEPING WITH THEM! If this sounds tough it is. SELF-FULLNESS is about living life. Don't throw yours away because you are afraid to ask someone to use a condom.

No Means NO!

And remember you can always say NO! Practice that now. Say NO! Again. Louder. Shout it out. Good. If you insist on a condom and your partner says no, then you say no! I know too many women who got themselves in trouble with unwanted pregnancies or worse because they "didn't want to hurt the guy's feelings" by insisting he wears a condom. Forget his feelings, protect your life! Any man who will not wear a condom when you ask him to does not respect you. A SELF-FULL person does not spend time with such people and neither should you. If your partner says no in the bedroom you can take my word for it that he or she will say no in other places too and your life together will be miserable.

Keep practicing saying NO! until doing so becomes second nature to you.

Exercise. No, thank you!

1. You can learn to become comfortable saying NO! by practicing it in a variety of non-threatening situations. Make a list of places or situations where you can practice saying no. For example, at the dry cleaners when the clerk asks you if you want extra starch? Or at the supermarket when the cashier asks you if you want help out to your car?

_____

_____

_____

_____

_____

_____

_____

_____

_____

_____

_____

2. After you have said NO! to someone, record how the experience felt to you.

_____

_____

_____

_____

_____

_____

_____

_____

_____

_____

3. Does saying NO! get easier over time? Why or why not?

_____

_____

_____

_____

_____

_____

_____

_____

_____

_____

If your answer was no, I encourage you to talk your difficulty over with someone. You may have some emotional blocks that are preventing from saying no. It would be very helpful to get rid of those blocks so you can take better care of yourself.

Saying "I Love You"

The three most powerful and yet misused words in the English language are "I love you". Tell the people you care about how much they mean to you and how much you appreciate having them in your life. Let the people you love know that you love them. Do not assume that they know. Tell them. Show them. It will benefit both of you.

"I love you" is also misused. Some people use it so freely that it has lost its special meaning. If you are one of those people refrain from using the phrase haphazardly. Tell the ones you truly love that you love them. Let the others know that you are fond of them, care about them, or like them a lot. Make your "I love you" words special. It will really pay off.

5

SELF-FULL HEALTH

I cannot emphasize enough the importance of good health in a SELF-FULL life. Good habits, regular medical examinations and daily health maintenance are key to a long and happy life. This chapter will support you in your efforts to improve and maintain your health, including, ways for you to kick your "bad health habits", such as smoking, excessive drinking, excessive eating, inactivity, and insomnia. These "bad habits" undermine any positive effort you may make towards improving your health.

The Importance of Self-Care

The only person responsible for your health is you. It is not the doctors. Or your therapist. Or your mother. It is you. Statistics tell us that more and more of us are being exposed to toxins and pollutants everyday. They are being found in our drinking water, in our food, and in our air. Cancer and heart disease are on the rise. As are systematic diseases such as lupus and AIDS. I am not reiterating these troublesome facts to frighten you. I am offering them to remind you of the importance of self-care.

Resistance and Fear

One of the many reasons why people don't go to the doctor is fear. Are you afraid of going to the doctor? When was the last time you had a physical? Let's explore your fears to see if we can dispel them so you can take better care of yourself.

On the surface it appears that many people are afraid of the doctor because they simply don't want to know the "bad news". They believe that if they don't know it will go away. We all know that this approach is irrational. If you are ill, you are ill and the only way to make it go away is to address it. However, if we take a closer look at this reason, we can find another more powerful, and somewhat more rational, reason underneath.

To help you understand this a bit more, I would like to introduce you to Rachel. She is a patient of mine, a woman in her early forties who hasn't been to the doctor in almost twenty years despite chronic back pain. The reason she won't go to the doctor is because she is afraid of what he will tell her. She is convinced that the pain in her back is a cancerous tumor. What Rachel is doing, and I see this over and over again in many of my patients, is displacing her anxieties over one area of her life onto her health. As long as she is focused on her health, she doesn't have to think about the bad marriage she is in or her estrangement from her eldest child. This phenomenon of displacing anxiety from one's life onto one's health is a common one. In the case of Rachel, once we addressed her anxieties and got them under control she was able to go to the doctor. I am delighted to report that the back pain she suffered from was not due to a tumor, but rather to her lack of physical activity and weak stomach muscles.

Does any of what I relayed about Rachel ring true for you? Could you be displacing anxiety as she is? If so, what are you really worried about? Keep in mind that anxiety is worry or fear about the future. Maybe if you can address your real concerns, your aches and pains and fears of the doctor will go away as they did with Rachel. To help you, try the following exercise.

Exercise. *Worry, Worry, Worry*

1. Write down your reasons for not going to the doctor, or taking your medicine, or whatever other health care task you are not performing.

_____

_____

_____

_____

_____

_____

_____

_____

_____

_____

_____

_____

2. Now, write down what problems you would think about, or focus your energies on if you were in perfect health.

_____

_____

_____

_____

_____

_____

_____

_____

_____

_____

_____

_____

3. Spend some time solving these real problems and the record whether your fears about the doctor and your health have changed.

_____
_____
_____
_____
_____
_____
_____
_____
_____
_____
_____
_____

SELF-FULL Health Checklist

Being SELF-FULL about your health means keeping up with annual and bi-annual appointments with your doctors and dentist. It also means taking as instructed any medication you may need. It means keeping the prescription on your eyeglasses current. It means wearing your eye glasses, hearing aids, or other aides as required.

Here is a checklist to help you stay on top of your health needs. There is space provided for you to add your personal health requirements.

- Dentist
- Mammogram
- Annual Physical
- Medication Compliance
- Eye care
- Pap Smear

- Blood pressure
- Cholesterol check
- Blood sugar test
- Stress test
- Breast exam
- Prostrate exam

What I need to do:

_____

_____

_____

_____

_____

_____

_____

_____

_____

Kicking Bad Habits

We live in a very fortunate time. There is so much we can do to take care of our health. We have tools and techniques available to us that were not available a generation ago. Let's take a look of some of them.

No Smoking

Doctor's tell us that the number one thing a person can do to improve their health is to "kick the habit". The cigarette habit that is. For those of you addicted to nicotine, giving up cigarettes has probably been the bane of your existence. If you are like most smokers, you have tried to quit more times than you can remember.

Like most addictions, there are two components to recovery. One is the physical component. The other is the psychological component. For cigarette smokers, the physical component is the nicotine. It has been scientifically proven that nicotine is addictive. Therefore any attempt to quit smoking must include a method of weaning yourself off of the nicotine. Ask your physician about the nicotine patches and other options that are available either by prescription or over-the-counter to address this part of your recovery.

The psychological component can be a bit more complicated. Smokers smoke because doing so satisfies some need (not just the need for nicotine). For most, smoking is a way to cope with stress and anxiety. They feel nervous, they light up. Too much work to do, take a cigarette break. To recover psychologically from a smoking addiction, you must identify the underlying need that is being served and find another way to meet it. For example, if you smoke because you are nervous, try relaxation exercises. If you smoke, because you are bored, take up a sport or hobby.

Exercise. *Kicking the Habit*

If smoking is your bad habit, what will you use to "kick the habit?" Record your plan here:

1. To address the physical component, I will:

_____
_____
_____
_____
_____
_____
_____
_____
_____
_____
_____

2. The psychological need(s) being met by my smoking is(are):

_____
_____
_____

_____

_____

_____

_____

_____

_____

_____

3. To meet those needs in a more healthful manner, I will:

_____

_____

_____

_____

_____

_____

_____

_____

_____

_____

Giving up the Bottle

My heart breaks for people caught in the trap of alcoholism. Not just the drinker, but also the family members and friends of the drinker. Alcoholism kills in so many ways. If you or someone you love has a drinking problem address it immediately. Left untreated, alcoholism kills the drinker and innocent people who get in their path.

If you are the one with the problem, I urge you to go to an Alcoholics Anonymous meeting soon. Their success rate is unbeatable. In addition, go into therapy. By combining the structure and support of AA with the insight of psychotherapy, you can break away from the hold alcohol has on your life.

If you love someone who has a problem, I urge you to go to Al-Anon. Al-Anon is a program like AA for the loved ones of alcoholics. At Al-Anon you will find support from others who are suffering as you are. You will also learn tools you can use to deal with the alcoholic in your life. The telephone numbers for both organizations can be found in your local phone book.

Living Binge-free

A binge is an episode of over-eating. I am not talking about Thanksgiving when everyone overeats! I am talking about a repeated pattern of overeating in response to emotional triggers.

To overcome binge eating, you must address the psychological reasons for why you overeat. Just like the smoker must determine what psychological needs are being met by his smoking, the overeater needs to find out when and why she overeats and then learn other ways to deal with those situations. There are many good books on the subject. You would also benefit enormously with the help of a competent psychotherapist who specializes in the treatment of binge eating. Groups psychotherapy is especially effective for this problem.

In Chapter Two SELF-FULL Eating, you did an exercise called "Emotional Eating." What did that exercise reveal about you? Are you an emotional eater? Did that exercise reveal patterns of behavior that you need to deal with? If so, try the next exercise to help you find other ways to cope with your life besides overeating.

Exercise. Overcoming Overeating

1. What patterns did the exercise "Emotional Eating" in Chapter Two reveal ?

_____

_____

_____

_____

_____

_____

_____

_____

_____

_____

2. Were you able to do anything about those patterns when you learned about them? Why or why not?

_____

_____

_____

_____

_____

_____

_____

_____

_____

_____

3. Keep a record of the foods you eat and the feelings you feel for another five days. This time include an entry identifying what else you could have done to deal with the feeling besides eat.

Food   Feeling   Substitute Activity

Day 1

_____

_____

_____

_____

_____

_____

_____

_____

_____

_____

_____

_____

Day 2

_____

_____

_____

_____

_____

_____

_____

_____

_____

_____

Day 3

_____

_____

_____

_____

_____

_____

_____

_____

_____
_____
_____

Day 4

_____
_____
_____
_____
_____
_____
_____
_____
_____
_____
_____

Day 5

_____
_____
_____
_____
_____
_____
_____
_____
_____
_____
_____
_____

4. Make a "master" list of all the things you can do instead of eating. Post your list in a prominent place in your home so you are use it easily. Here are some ideas to get you started.

Master List

Take a walk	Read a book	Call a friend
Cry	Sew a button	Watch TV
Wash your car	Rent a movie	Write a letter
Have shower	Soak in the tub	Laugh
Yell into a pillow	Go shopping	Play with the dog

_____
_____
_____
_____
_____
_____
_____
_____
_____
_____

Overcoming the Couch-Potato Syndrome

Chapter Three SELF-FULL Fitness addressed the benefits of regular exercise. Are you still not convinced? Are you still sitting on your couch? Let's find out why.

Exercise. *Baby It's Cold Outside…and Other Excuses*

1. What are your reasons (read "excuses!") for not exercising regularly?

_____
_____

_____
_____
_____
_____
_____
_____
_____
_____
_____
_____

2. What are the benefits to you for continuing to be a couch potato?

_____
_____
_____
_____
_____
_____
_____
_____
_____
_____

3. What are the costs?

_____
_____
_____
_____
_____
_____
_____
_____

_____
_____
_____

4. Are your reasons really "reasons" or are they "excuses"? If they are excuses, argue against them here.

_____
_____
_____
_____
_____
_____
_____
_____
_____
_____
_____

If you are still not budging, re-read Chapter Three. If that doesn't get you moving, I give up. Stay put, but don't complain to anyone if you are tired all the time, can't fit into your clothes, and have no fun in your life.

Sleeping Like a Baby

To sleep like a baby, you need to rely on the science of sleep hygiene. Sleep hygiene offers solutions to many restless nights sleep. Here are ten suggestions that should help you get your zzz's.

· Keep your bedroom free from stress. Use your bedroom for sleeping only. Do not eat, drink, work, or watch TV in your bedroom. You need to associate your bedroom with sleep only to get a restful night.

· Cut out the caffeine. That means no coffee, tea, sodas, or chocolate. Check your medications. Many over the counter medications contain caffeine. Cut those out too. Caffeine is a stimulant and can keep you up at night even if you consume it in the morning.

· Don't exercise more than four hours before bed. Exercising late in the day can stimulate your system, making it difficult to fall asleep.

· Watch the news in the morning rather than in the evening. The stress of the daily news can keep you up at night. So can the glimmer of the television screen. Keep the TV off if you want to sleep throughout the night.

· Stop drinking several hours before going to sleep so you don't need to wake in the middle of the night to empty your bladder.

· Don't eat late at night either. Digestion can also keep you from sound sleep.

· End your day with a warm bath or shower or some relaxing music. You want to soothe yourself before you sleep so you can ease into slumber.

· Make certain that your bed, sheets and blankets are comfortable.

· Make certain that the temperature in your room is comfortable for you too. Too hot or too cold can disrupt sleep. If you are sleeping with someone whose temperature needs are different than yours, try to balance out the difference with extra blankets and open windows.

If you can't fall asleep after ten minutes or so, get out of bed and out of the bedroom. Go to another area of your home an engage in a stress-free activity until you feel sleepy enough to try again.

A Word about HIV and other STD's

Sadly we live in a world where we need to protect ourselves from deadly communicative diseases. The most serious one we are facing right now is AIDS, the autonomic immune deficiency syndrome. AIDS is causes by a virus known as the HIV virus. The virus is transmitted through the exchange of bodily fluids, such as blood, saliva, and semen. It is imperative if you are sexually active that you are regularly checked for the AIDS virus. It is a simple blood test that could save your life. For more information, ask you physician, or if you prefer complete anonymity, contact a health clinic in your area. This is one area of your health where ignorance can truly kill you. Be SELF-FULL and know the complete status of your health.

There are other sexually transmitted diseases (STD's) that you need to protect yourself from. They include herpes, gonorrhea, chlamydial infections, and syphilis. To protect yourself, quiz your partner about their sexual history. Insist on testing if you have concerns, and always, always, always, use a condom.

There is one more sexually transmitted condition that needs mentioning, and that is pregnancy. Consult with your physician about the appropriate method for you to use to prevent an unwanted pregnancy. And, remember, always, always, always, use a condom.

Can We Talk? The Benefits of Psychotherapy

I know that many people are afraid of psychotherapists. My experience has been that it is the braver, stronger, healthier people who find their way into a therapist office. The truth is we all need someone to talk to. Someone who will listen without judgment or criticism. Sure you can talk to your friends, but after a while even the best friends can't hear your story anymore! But a good therapist can. She can listen over and over again for as long as you need to tell your story and get relief from your problems. I strongly urge you to find a therapist whom you like and feel comfortable with and see her regularly. It can make a world of difference in how you see yourself and how you live your life.

If you really want to change your personal relationships I urge you to join a psychotherapy group. Find one run by a trained group psychotherapist and you will receive enormous benefits from your therapeutic work. In "group" you will learn how to interact better with people and how to improve your relationships overall.

Who's Who? How to Pick a Therapist

Once you decide to go into therapy it is important for you to find a therapist who you like and feel comfortable with. You are welcome to "shop around" for a therapist. Interview several to help you decide who you want to work with. My recommendation is that you work with a licensed therapist, although if money is an issue, you can get some good therapy from student interns training to become therapists. Check your local universities and colleges for interns who are available for a reduced fee.

To find a good therapist there are several ways to proceed. You can ask your physician for a referral. You can call the local chapter of the American Psychological Association or other professional associations and they will refer you to a licensed person in your area. Or, you can refer to the Yellow pages or local newspapers.

To help clarify who is who, let me give you brief description of the types of therapist around and what their credentials are. To begin with there are psychiatrists. Psychiatrists are medical doctors trained in psychiatry. As a general statement, most people seen by psychiatrists are treated with medication. Some psychiatrist do psychotherapy so ask when you make your initial appointment. Then there are psychologists. Psychologists hold Ph.D. or Psy.D. degrees in psychology and are formally trained in the art of psychotherapy. Psychologists do not prescribe medication. Licensed at the Master degree level are social workers and marriage and family counselors. Marriage and family counselors in particular are trained to do psychotherapy but do not have as much formal education or training as psychologists do.

The requirement for licensure as a psychologist or psychotherapist vary in each state. Check with the American Psychological Association for more information.

6

SELF-FULL CAREER

Are you dissatisfied with your professional life? Do you have a professional life? Do you want a professional life? If having a satisfying professional life is something you desire, this chapter will help you focus on the most SELF-FULL career for you.

Deciding on a career is not a task for your brain. It is really a task for your heart. To choose SELF-FULL work, work that will give you joy, self-esteem, a sense of accomplishment, and financial rewards, you must choose from your heart. Too many professional lives have been wasted by decisions made from the head. Take Louis for example. Louis spent eighteen miserable years as an accountant. He became an accountant because being an accountant was a "smart thing to do." It was a stable, respectable profession that could earn Louis a good living. The problem was that Louis was really a people person not a numbers person. Eighteen years later, Louis acknowledged for the first time that his heart always told him to be a teacher. So, he followed his heart, got his teaching credential and became a high school teacher. He is happy, healthier, and more fulfilled now than ever before. Becoming a teacher was a SELF-FULL action for Louis and it has made a huge difference in his life. Finding your SELF-FULL career can do the same for you.

Choosing Work That Fits YOU!

The key to finding your SELF-FULL career is in choosing work that fits you, not somebody else.

Exercise. Questions and Answers

These are very thought provoking questions. They are intended to get your heart involved in this process. There are no right or wrong answers, only your answers. So take your time and think about your responses. Come back to this exercise over time to expand upon or change your responses. Remember this is a process and through it all you are evolving and changing and becoming more SELF-FULL.

1. What do you really want out of life? Is it joy and happiness? Money? Family? To make a difference?

_____

_____

_____

_____

_____

_____

_____

_____

_____

_____

_____

2. If you could give anything to the world what would it be? A monument? A book? More love? A future President?

_____

_____

_____

_____
_____
_____
_____
_____
_____
_____
_____

3. What issues, concerns, or situations are important to you? The environment? Peace? Space travel?

_____
_____
_____
_____
_____
_____
_____
_____
_____
_____

4. What topics hold your interest? Current events? History? Art? Gossip? Cooking tips? Exercise?

_____
_____
_____
_____
_____
_____

_____

_____

_____

_____

_____

5. What do you love to do, talk about, think about, read about? Gardening? Politics? The stock market? Your children?

_____

_____

_____

_____

_____

_____

_____

_____

_____

_____

6. What could you see yourself devoting time and energy to? Your family? Saving the whales? Growing the perfect rose?

_____

_____

_____

_____

_____

_____

_____

_____

_____

_____

7. Is there any particular group of people with whom you feel the most affinity? empathy? sympathy? understanding?

_____

_____

_____

_____

_____

_____

_____

_____

_____

_____

_____

Deciding What to Do

Did you know that a lot of the time our most SELF-FULL career choices presented themselves when we were children but we or those around us never paid attention? To continue your journey of deciding what to do, revisit your childhood dreams and activities. They are often a window into the soul of your career.

Exercise. Childhood Treasures

Think back to when you were a child and answer the following questions.

1. What did YOU want to be when you grew up?

_____

_____

_____
_____
_____
_____
_____
_____
_____
_____
_____
_____

2. Which activities filled most of your spare time?

_____
_____
_____
_____
_____
_____
_____
_____
_____
_____
_____

3. Which subjects did you enjoy most in school?

_____
_____
_____
_____
_____
_____
_____

_____

_____

_____

4. Which subjects did you excel in?

_____

_____

_____

_____

_____

_____

_____

_____

_____

In doing this exercise, I hope some fond memories came back to you. Did you learn anything interesting about your career aspirations? Did anything helpful reveal itself? Record your observations here.

_____

_____

_____

_____

_____

_____

_____

_____

_____

_____

The next part of this particular journey is to focus on your unique gifts and talents. Skills are less important. They can be learned.

Exercise. *That's easy!*

1. What comes naturally to you? Speaking in public? Doing math calculations? Fixing electronic items?

_____

_____

_____

_____

_____

_____

_____

_____

_____

_____

2. What do you most enjoy doing? Thinking about? Learning about? Playing with your computer? Painting? Listening to music? Singing?

_____

_____

_____

_____

_____

_____

_____

_____

_____

_____

3. Have you ever lost yourself in an activity? By that I mean, have you ever been so involved with what you were doing that you lost all track of time? When was that? What were you doing?

_____
_____
_____
_____
_____
_____
_____
_____
_____
_____
_____

You have spent quite a bit of time now exploring the areas that will lead you to your SELF-FULL career. What have you learned? Did any ideas present themselves to you? If so, what are you going to do about it? Record your ideas here.

_____
_____
_____
_____
_____
_____
_____
_____
_____
_____
_____

Turning Ideas into Careers

Turning your list of ideas into a satisfying career will require a bit more work on your part. Now it's time to do some homework. Take your list of ideas to the library and start researching the careers that your ideas inspire. In the reference section, you will find volume after volume of books listing all the jobs people are doing.

Next, peruse the classified section of you newspaper. Start with the A's and read through to the Z's and circle anything and everything that you might be interested in. Notice how many different jobs there are and how many different industries there are to do them.

Then, start talking to people who are doing the kind of work you are thinking about doing. Make an appointment and interview them. Ask them what a day in their work life is like. Find out how they got started. Ask them for suggestions on how you too can start.

Find books in your library or bookstore on jobs in the fields you are interested in. Take notes. The ideas will start flowing. Follow them.

If you want to checkout your new career before committing to it, take a class in it. Or, find part-time position and see what you learn. If part-time is unavailable, volunteer to get inside the door.

There are career counselors, job banks, employment offices and headhunters out there to help you. Call them. Meet with them. Find out your options.

Remember to keep checking in with yourself. What feels right? Follow your heart and you will find your way. I hope these words have started your ideas flowing. What step can you take next to get started? Here's a place for you to jot it down. Good luck.

Exercise. What's Next…

Here's what I'll do next in pursuit of my SELF-FULL career:

_____

_____

_____
_____
_____
_____
_____
_____
_____
_____
_____
_____

Success on the Job

Now that you have figured out (or almost figured out) your SELF-FULL career, let's take at a look at how you can make the most of it!

Here are six keys to success on the job that I learned from some people "in the know":

· Show up earlier and leave later than your boss.

· Have a daily plan of activities and execute it.

· Always do what you say you will do. Do not make promises you cannot keep. It is better to say no than to be a people-pleaser by saying yes and then not following through.

· Take complete responsibility for all that you do. That includes taking credit for what you do well and apologizing for what you do wrong.

· Always be polite and courteous. And,

· Keep a smile on your face and make eye contact.

By applying the skills you are learning through your SELF-FULLNESS journey, your success up the career ladder is practically guaranteed! Happy climbing!

7

SELF-FULL GROOMING

Taking care of yourself is not just about speaking your mind or finding the right job, it is also about taking good care of how you look. This part can be a lot of fun. This chapter will take you through a complete makeover. We will start with the top of your head and end in your closet! Of course, please remember the ideas I am about to present are only for your consideration. You are the ultimate authority over what you wear and how you look.

Let us start with some basic questions about where you are now in terms of your personal grooming. Your answers will guide you in deciding what if anything you want to change or improve.

Exercise. Mirror, Mirror

1. How happy are you with your current appearance?

_____

_____

_____

_____

_____

_____

_____
_____
_____
_____
_____

2. What about yourself would you like to be different?

_____
_____
_____
_____
_____
_____
_____
_____
_____
_____
_____

3. Of the things you would like to be different which ones are realistic? In other words, if you are 5 feet 3 inches tall and you would prefer to be 5 feet 10 inches tall, well that is unrealistic. But if you have brown hair and would prefer to have blond hair, that's a possibility.

_____
_____
_____
_____
_____
_____
_____
_____

_____
_____

4. Of the realistic differences you would like, what changes could you make to bring those differences to life?

_____
_____
_____
_____
_____
_____
_____
_____
_____
_____
_____

So, what did your answers reveal? If you are happy with who you are now, good for you. You can skip the following few pages and move ahead. On the other hand, if there are things that you would like to improve, take a look at the ideas set forth in this chapter. Maybe they can help you be all that you want to be.

Head-to-Toe Makeover

Let's get started with your "crowning glory", your hair.

Hair

A big mistake that many women make is trying to wear a hairstyle that just doesn't suit their facial features, skin type, eye color, or physical characteristics. The most SELF-FULL way to wear your hair is as close to natural as you can get. That goes for color as well as style. For men, a neat clean haircut and trimmed facial hair usually work well.

Look through magazines and catalogs for styles you like. Show the styles to a professional stylist for their input. Choose a style that is not only flattering but also easy to care for. Remember you need to be able to recreate the style when you are on your own.

Make-up

If you wear make-up, here are some tips to make makeup quick and easy. Remember that less is definitely more. You want people to notice you, not your makeup.

Start with a concealer and cover up any blemishes or dark circles you may have under your eyes. Choose a color that closely matches your skin tone. Too often women choose a concealer that is too light and actually draw more attention to their "trouble" areas.

If you choose to you can add a foundation. Make certain that it goes on sheer and matches your the skin tones. Blend the foundation under your chin and into the beginning of your neck area.

The third "basic" is your blush. Choose a tone that matches the color in your cheeks when you exercise. For most women that will be a pink or coral color. All you want to do is give your skin a rosy glow. You do not want streaks of color running across your face.

The fourth step is to apply a neutral eye shadow. Try a brown or taupe color. They are the most natural. For heaven's sake stay away from blue!

Coat your lashes with either black or brown mascara. Use several coats to darken and thicken your lashes. Separate lumped lashes with a lash comb. Stay away from false eyelashes and colored mascara. They may be fine for special occasions but they are not good for everyday use.

Lastly, go for a sheer neutral lipstick or gloss.

Try these "tricks" of the trade to start. Add your own ideas as you go along. One last tip, keep your makeup applicators clean. Never share them. If you want to share makeup use clean cotton swabs as applicators. Use a new one each time you dip into your makeup color.

Here are some suggestions on how you can save money on your cosmetic purchases: use perfumed lotion instead of the actual perfume; have your makeup done at a cosmetics counter; use multi-purpose products, such as moisturizers that contain sunscreen; and sample new products with travel sizes rather than full sizes.

Bodyworks

Be nice to your skin. It is what protects you from the harsh elements of the sun and sky. Moisturize daily and apply sunscreen every time you walk out the door.

Hands and Nails

Did you know that the area on a body that shows age the most is your hands? It's true. What do your hands say about you? Keep your hands and nails moisturized. I like to keep a bottle of moisturizer near each sink in my home. Each time I wash my hands I rub in a little moisturizer. It is an easy way to keep my hands soft. Apply sunscreen to the back of your hands every time you go out.

Well-manicured hands always look good. Whether you wear your nails long or short, keep them neat and healthy with regular care. Whenever you wear colored polish on your nails, especially red, carry the bottle of polish with you for quick touch ups. Nothing ruins a pretty appearance like chipped nail polish.

Feet Care

Your feet carry you everywhere you go, be kind to them. Treat them to warm soaks, soothing lotions, and regular pedicures. Wear the right shoe size. Your feet continue to grow as you age. Pregnancy can change you foot size too. Try not to be sensitive to the number on the box. Wear a size that fits you. Forcing your feet into shoes that are too small can result in blisters and other foot problems. If you have a foot problem, see a podiatrist. They are doctors specially trained to deal with the feet.

Clothes that Make the Grade

Does your wardrobe need updating? Does it reflect the you you want to project to the world? Does it reflect the you you feel you are? Maybe it is time for a wardrobe makeover.

Color Yourself Beautiful

It is actually quite easy to have a nice wardrobe. Most women shop on impulse. They see something they like and they buy it. They end up with a closet full of clothes that don't really work together and they constantly complain that they have nothing to wear. The secret to building a successful wardrobe is knowing what colors and styles work for you and build a basic wardrobe from there. Then you can add pieces to your basic wardrobe as accessories or special items as you desire.

There are two important elements to your SELF-FULL wardrobe: your basic colors and your accent colors. Your basic colors are the colors that form the foundation of your wardrobe. Your "fundamentals" will be in your basic colors. What are your "fundamentals?" For women, they are your blazers, slacks, skirts, and dresses. For men, they are a sports jacket, a pair of dress slacks, a pair of casual slacks, a business suit, and a tuxedo. Basic colors include white or cream and black, brown, navy, or gray. Go to your favorite department store and play a little. Try on these basic colors are decide for yourself which ones work for you. Choose between white or cream as your basic light color and then choose two dark colors among black, brown, navy and gray. Your wardrobe basics should include a blazer, dress, skirt, blouse, and pair of slacks in each of your dark basic and light colors.

Exercise. Knowing the Basics

1. What basic colors did you choose for yourself? Mark them down here.

_____

_____

_____

_____

_____

_____

_____

_____

_____

_____

_____

2. Do you have your "fundamentals" in each of your basic colors? If not, what is missing? Over time you can add to your wardrobe by filling in the missing pieces.

_____

_____

_____

_____

_____

_____

_____

_____

_____

_____

_____

Once you have gotten your basic colors worked out, you add some splash and style to your wardrobe with your accent colors. Accent colors can be anything that looks fabulous and makes you feel fabulous. Some great accent colors are red, pink, and green. Find the shade or shades that suit you and fill in your wardrobe with blouses, scarves, and sweaters in those colors.

Exercise. *Shades of Color*

Let's go through the same exercise for your accent colors as you did for your basic colors.

1. What accents colors did you choose?

_____

_____

_____

_____

_____

_____

_____

_____

_____

_____

_____

2. Do you have a shirt, scarf or tie , and sweater in each of your accent colors? If not, what is missing? Fill in your wardrobe with extra splashes of your accent colors when you can.

_____

_____

_____

_____

_____

_____

_____

_____

_____

_____

_____

As far as shoes, handbags, and other accessories go, stick to your basic colors again and get some in each color. Try to always wear the same color handbag, belt and shoes for a really "put together" look.

Accent your outfit with interesting pieces of costume or real jewelry. Try to keep your metals the same. For example, stick to silver jewelry when your outfit has silver buttons on in it.

These little suggestions go a long way to help you create your most SELF-FULL look. Once you get the hang of these ideas you will see that deciding what to wear becomes easy and fun.

Lingerie

Did your mother or grandmother always remind you to wear clean underwear every time you left the house in case you had an accident? They were not completely wrong! While I disagree with their concern about having an accident, I do agree with the value in wearing nice undergarments. There is very little that can make a woman feel as pretty and confident as wearing attractive undergarments. Treat yourself to a set of pretty lace bra and panties and see for yourself whether they make a difference in how you feel about yourself.

Exercise. Shopping Spree

1. Go through your wardrobe and make a list of what basic pieces are missing.

_____
_____
_____
_____
_____
_____
_____
_____
_____
_____

2. Carry the list with you. If you see a sale, you can take advantage of it and come home with items you can really use, instead of merely more stuff to clutter your closet. Record your purchases here.

_____
_____
_____
_____
_____
_____
_____
_____
_____
_____

Neatness Counts

Lastly, I want to address neatness. By neatness, I am referring to having a neat appearance. A neat appearance means that loose buttons are tightened, hanging threads are removed, wrinkled shirts are ironed, chipped nail polish is fixed up, scuffed shoes are polished, and tears are mended. Paying attention to little details like this says a lot about how you feel about yourself. It is a reflection of high self-esteem and I encourage you to practice tending to these details on a regular basis.

8

SELF-FULL AT HOME

Being SELF-FULL is not just about taking care of how you look and what you do. It is also about where and how you live. Since we took a look at what was hanging in your closets in Chapter Seven, let's tackle the rest of your home in this chapter. Your surroundings are a reflection of who you are. Let them shine!

What do your surroundings say about you? Here's an exercise to help you find out.

Exercise. Home Run

1. Is your home decorated in a style that you enjoy? If yes, what is that style? If not, what style would you prefer?

_____

_____

_____

_____

_____

_____

_____

_____

_____

_____

_____

2. Do the colors and furnishing suit you? If not, what would work better?

_____

_____

_____

_____

_____

_____

_____

_____

_____

_____

3. Is your home pleasing to come home to? Why or why not?

_____

_____

_____

_____

_____

_____

_____

_____

_____

_____

4. Do you feel "at home" when you are there? If not, what would make it "homier"?

_____
_____
_____
_____
_____
_____
_____
_____
_____
_____
_____

5. Do you feel safe at home? If not, what is missing? What do you need to feel safe? A security system? A dog? Extra lights? Extra locks? A roommate?

_____
_____
_____
_____
_____
_____
_____
_____
_____
_____
_____

Clutter, Clutter Everywhere

Let's talk about clutter. One patient of mine referred to the clutter in her home as "soiling the nest." We shared many laughs over that phrase, but it is not too far from the truth. If your home is cluttered, messy, and/or dirty you too are "soiling the nest." In reality, you are soiling your home. Do you enjoy living in a mess? If you do, that's fine. You are "allowed"! But if you do not, we need to take a look at why you allow that condition to continue and what you can do to make it better.

Exercise. *Getting Rid of the Mess*

To get rid of clutter take the following steps:

1. Go through your closets and ask yourself these simple questions for each item you come across:
   · Have I used this item in the last year?
   · Will I use it in the next year?
   · Do I love it so I cannot part with it?
   · Is it irreplaceable?

Use this space to make notes to help you along.

_____

_____

_____

_____

_____

_____

_____

_____

_____

_____

2. If you answer no to the above questions, throw the item out. Or, if you cannot do that give it away. Or, if you cannot do that, have a sale. What are you going to do?

_____

_____

_____

_____

_____

_____

_____

_____

_____

_____

_____

3. When you have finished the closets, attend to the drawers. Which drawers need your attention?

_____

_____

_____

_____

_____

_____

_____

_____

_____

_____

4. After the drawers, tackle your spare bedrooms, basement, garage or any other place you collect things. What will you tackle next?

_____

_____

_____

_____

_____

_____

_____

_____

_____

_____

_____

Here is a suggested rule-of-thumb for papers. Make it a habit to never touch a piece of paper more than once. The first time you look at it decide where it goes and put it there. Moving it from pile to pile only takes up valuable time and adds to your clutter.

Going through your clutter this way is one of the most empowering tasks you can undertake. It can be immediately motivating and give you quite a sense of control.

The BIG Clean Up

When you can afford it, hire yourself a cleaning person. Invite that person into your home once or twice a month to help with the more difficult cleaning chores, like cleaning the windows or the inside of the refrigerator. Budget it into your monthly expenses. You deserve it. To do so is SELF-FULL. Besides, you are giving someone else a job and helping them with their SELF-FULLNESS too!

Perk-Up

There are little ways for you to make your home more appealing. Fresh flowers always brighten up a room. Soft background music can create a relaxing, inviting atmosphere. Throw pillows add color and pizzazz. It doesn't have to cost a lot of money either. Garage and rummage sales are great places to pick up little odds and ends to brighten up your room. A coat of paint can do wonders, as can a new comforter on your bed. What can you do to perk up your place?

Exercise. Home Sweet Home

1. In what ways can you add a little pizzazz to your home?

_____

_____

_____

_____

_____

_____

_____

_____

_____

_____

_____

2. What do you need to do to make them happen?

_____

_____

_____

_____

_____

_____

_____

_____

_____

_____

_____

3. Pick one and do it soon. Which one did you pick?

_____

_____

_____

_____

_____

_____

_____

_____

_____

_____

Exercise. The "To Do" List

Now that you've taken a good close look at your home, take a moment to write down what needs to be done to shape up your home so it reflects the SELF-FULL you.

1. The list.

                    My "To Do" List

_____

_____

_____

_____

_____

_____

_____

_____

_____

_____

_____

2. Put a number in front of each item on your list to reflect the order in which you will pursue doing it. Which one was first? When will you get started?

_____

_____

_____

_____

_____

_____

_____

_____

_____

_____

_____

9

SELF-FULL FINANCES

SELF-FULLNESS with regard to money and finance means meeting your needs now and preparing for your future. It means being fiscally responsible. This chapter will show you how.

You deserve money and financial security. In order to have the money you deserve you need to be "business like." You need to be able to set aside your emotions and become practical. For example, you can set up a financial structure to assist you with your goals. Or you can become more self sufficient and self reliant when it comes to money matters. Perhaps you need to be more willing to spend money on yourself or to earn more money, a lot more money. How about taking classes and seminars to teach you what you don't already know?

Money Matters

It doesn't matter where you are financially right now. What matters is that you start now to take charge of your finances. You can start anywhere. Does your checkbook need balancing? Do it. Have you got a savings account? No, open one. Are you making the maximum contribution to your company's 401K plan? If not, make an appointment to see the financial officer at your company and sign up. What can you do to start taking charge of your finances?

Exercise. *Charge It!*

1. Begin by gathering all of your financial papers, such as, check stubs, tax returns, credit card receipts, etc. What shape are your papers in? Do they need better organizing? If so, get a small file box and a dozen or so file folders. Create a file folder for each category of paper you have and start filing! Describe the state of your affairs here.

_____

_____

_____

_____

_____

_____

_____

_____

_____

_____

2. Once your papers are organized, take a good look at them. What needs your attention? Does a bill need paying? List here what you need to do to get your financial self in better shape.

_____

_____

_____

_____

_____

_____

_____

_____
_____
_____

3. Pick one item at a time off your list and do it! Which one will you do first?

_____
_____
_____
_____
_____
_____
_____
_____
_____
_____
_____

Conquering Your Fears

Did the above exercise make you anxious? Are you afraid of your finances? If you are, take heart so are many people. For some reason, money is a very frightening subject. Before we move on, let's study this notion of fear for a bit. Maybe I can help dispel some of your fears so you can become financially prosperous.

Fears is sometimes thought of as " false evidence appearing real." In other words, something seems real but when you take a closer look at it is isn't. Imagine a thump in the night. You become frighten. Why? Because you believe that the thump means a prowler is entering your home. In fact, it is only a tree branch hitting your window. You are afraid because you thought false evidence (the thump) was real (a prowler). Are you doing the same thing with money?

Exercise. *Things that go Thump in the Night*

1. What fears do you have about money? That there isn't enough? That you can't earn more? That you are not smart enough to handle it? Record your fears here.

_____

_____

_____

_____

_____

_____

_____

_____

_____

_____

2. Of the fears you just described, what is real and what is false?

Real:

_____

_____

_____

_____

_____

_____

_____

_____

_____

_____

False:

_____

_____

_____

_____

_____

_____

_____

_____

_____

_____

_____

3. Can your fears be described as "false evidence appearing real?" How so?

_____

_____

_____

_____

_____

_____

_____

_____

_____

_____

_____

When you overcome your fear of any problem, you gain control over it. It no longer controls you and you are well on your way to resolving it.

4. If your fears are not real, can you let go of them and move on? Why or why not?

_____

_____

_____

_____

_____

_____

_____

_____

_____

_____

The Ostrich Syndrome

One way that people who are afraid of money deal with money is by not dealing with it. I refer to this phenomenon as "The Ostrich Syndrome". People are figuratively burying their heads in the sand when it comes to money. That's fine and dandy if you can afford to do so, but most of us can't. Most of us need to pay attention to our finances or eventually we won't have any.

If you are an ostrich, let me help get your head out of the sand. The information that follows should help you gain some confidence in the area of finance and allow you to start paying attention.

Family Roots

Being comfortable with money has its root in the family. Some families speak openly about finances. Others are very secretive. Some families have a lot of money and are stingy and fearful. Other families have every little money and yet are generous and charitable. What kind of family do you come from?

Exercise. All in The Family

1. Describe in as much detail as you can your family's attitude toward money.

_____

_____

_____

_____

_____

_____

_____

_____

_____

_____

_____

2. Is your attitude towards money similar or dissimilar to your family's?

_____

_____

_____

_____

_____

_____

_____

_____

_____

_____

_____

3. Describe the attitude toward money that you would like to have.

_____

_____

_____

_____

_____

_____

_____

_____

_____

_____

_____

Your Financial Toolbox

Covering the basis of SELF-FULL finances includes having the following in place: a good credit rating, a checking account in your name, a savings account in your name, two to six months worth of living expenses tucked away in the case of an emergency, health insurance, life insurance (if you have dependents), car insurance (if you own a car), property insurance (if you own a home or condo), and a retirement account (regardless of your employment status.)

I recommend that these financial "necessities" become your first financial goals. Once you have all of these in place, you can move on to building wealth.

Exercise. *Covering the Basics*

1. Do you have these financial necessities in place?

_____

_____

_____

_____

_____

_____

_____

_____
_____
_____
_____

2. Which ones do you need?

_____
_____
_____
_____
_____
_____
_____
_____
_____
_____

3. What will you do to get what you are missing?

_____
_____
_____
_____
_____
_____
_____
_____
_____
_____

Checks and Balances

Just like our government, you need a system of checks and balances to keep your finances straight, starting with your checkbook balances. Get into the habit of balancing your checkbook every time your statement comes. It only takes a few minutes to reconcile your balance and to catch any errors. This will go a long way in helping you avoid unnecessary overdraft or other charges.

Another important part of your system is keeping your paperwork organized. In the exercise *Charge It!* I instructed you to create a filing system. As you can imagine, a filing system is only as effective as the filer. Get into the habit of filing papers away as soon as you receive them. Remember the suggestion I made in Chapter Eight, SELF-FULLNESS At Home, that you only touch a piece of paper once? Here is an example of where you can apply that suggestion. Once a bill, for example, comes into your home, act on it. Prepare the remittance slip for payment and put the bill itself into its place in your file box. Done!

To facilitate this process, I also recommend "the calendar system." Get yourself one of those small desk calendars that has a page for each day. When you receive a bill, prepare it for payment right away. Place the stamped, sealed envelop (with the check inside) into your calendar on the day you need to mail the payment for it be timely, then forget about it. Each day, turn the page of your calendar and mail the envelops that are stashed there. If you adopt this system you will never be late paying a bill again!

Getting Rich

Millionaires share that there are three elements to getting rich: spending less than you earn, investing cautiously, and preparing for the future. We will explore all three.

Living within Your Means

Living within your means implies that your spending habits match your earnings. If you are spending more than you earn in any given period, you are living outside your means. Living outside your means results in debt and an inability to accumulate wealth.

Let's take a look at your spending habits to see if you are living inside or outside your means.

Exercise. Balancing Act

1. How much money do you earn in a month from all sources (include alimony, investment interest, etc.)?

_____

_____

_____

_____

_____

_____

_____

_____

_____

_____

_____

2. How much money do you spend in a month (include everything, even change for the parking meter)? If you are not sure, keep track for a month and then return to this exercise.

_____

_____

_____

_____

_____

_____

_____

_____

_____

_____

3. If your earnings exceed your spending, consider yourself SELF-FULL and earmark the difference for investing. If your spending exceeds your earnings, identify where you can cut down your expenses to turn things around.

_____

_____

_____

_____

_____

_____

_____

_____

_____

_____

Avoiding Credit Card Debt

The single most effective thing you can do to accumulate wealth rich is to avoid credit card debt. The interest rates credit cards charge on unpaid balances will eat up any extra income you may earn. If you have credit card debt make it a priority to pay it off as quickly as possible and then vow never to get yourself in that situation again. Also investigate why you got into debt in the first place. The following exercise will offer some guidance.

Exercise. Debt Analysis

1. Where does your problem lie? Are your charging your rent or extra shoes on your credit cards?

_____

_____

_____

_____

_____

_____

_____

_____

_____

_____

_____

2. Does your problem reflect your living beyond your means? Are you underpaid? Under-employed?

_____

_____

_____

_____

_____

_____

_____

_____

_____

_____

_____

3. Do you need to supplement your income to meet your expenses? As you know, being SELF-FULL means being responsible for yourself. If

you need another job to makes ends meet, get another job. If you are underemployed, find a new job. Do whatever it takes to get out of debt and stay out. What will you do to help yourself?

_____

_____

_____

_____

_____

_____

_____

_____

_____

_____

_____

Basics of Investing 101

Once you are living debt free and your earnings exceed your expenses you are ready to start accruing wealth. Investing is the way to go.

Investing is not as hard as you think it is. Investing is actually easily understood if you take the time to educate yourself. Once you get started, investing is really about maintenance. The key is to get started NOW—wherever you are in your life. It is never too early or too late.

To be a successful investor think in terms of growth rather than quick rich schemes.

As for what type of investment to make, there are as many options as there are dollar bills floating around, but don't let that scare you. Once again, all you need is a little bit of education. There are hundreds of books and seminars available for you to educate yourself but beware these books and seminars are a lot like diet books and seminars, everyone who has had some success thinks that he has "the formula" for success. There is no one formula for everyone just like there is not one diet for everyone. Read and choose the one that fits for you.

Probably your best investment to get started with will be in the stock market. Over time the stock market has out performed most other forms of investing. The long-term trend in the market is for upward growth, despite occasional lapses or crashes. A stock is a share of ownership in a company. Buy stock in a company that you believe in, that you have faith in, and that has a history of good steady growth. Stay away from "hot" stocks or others that promise quick gains. Your investment strategy should be about long term growth not short-term profit. If you want short-term profit, take a road trip to Las Vegas or Atlantic City and try your luck. Or buy a lottery ticket. The stock market is not where you gamble it is where you earn if you are patient.

In deciding your investment strategies, you need to take a look at your goals and your personality. Why your personality? Because you need to understand your relationship to risk.

Exercise. Investment Goals

Take a few minutes to think about your financial goals.

1. Are you thinking about retirement or a new house? Do you need a new car or some new furniture? Do you want to be wealthy or comfortable? Write your thoughts here.

_____
_____
_____
_____
_____
_____
_____
_____
_____

_____
_____

2. Now examine what you wrote. Are you goals short or long term? Are they pressing or can they wait? Your answers will help you later on when you decide how and where to invest.

_____
_____
_____
_____
_____
_____
_____
_____
_____
_____

3. If you are young and have time to allow your money to work for you, you will be interested in growth. If you are older and/or need money to live on, chances are you will be looking for income producing investments. Which type of investment do your needs call for?

_____
_____
_____
_____
_____
_____
_____
_____

_____

_____

Exercise. *Me and My Shadow*

Now it is time to look at your tolerance for risk. Ask yourself the following questions and answer them as truthfully as you can. Doing so will save a lot of worry and fear later on.

1. How comfortable are you with risk? Describe yourself when it comes to this issue.

_____
_____
_____
_____
_____
_____
_____
_____
_____
_____
_____

2. Do you enjoy black diamonds ski runs or horse drawn sleigh rides? Why?

_____
_____
_____
_____
_____
_____
_____

_____
_____
_____

3. Do you worry if you don't have money in the bank to pay your bills on time? Why or why not?

_____
_____
_____
_____
_____
_____
_____
_____
_____
_____
_____

4. Can you sleep at night not knowing the answer to a question or does it keep you up? What do you tell yourself about the situation?

_____
_____
_____
_____
_____
_____
_____
_____
_____
_____

5. So, what did you learn about yourself?

_____

_____

_____

_____

_____

_____

_____

_____

_____

_____

_____

Another key to successful investing is diversification. Diversification simply means having your investment money divided among a variety of different types of investments. For example, you may have some of your money in stocks, some of it in a money market account, and the rest in bonds. One simple suggestion I once learned was to place money into a mutual fund. A mutual fund is an investment vehicle which invests in a variety of companies at once. You make a single investment into the fund and the fund manager invests the fund into the variety of companies. In other words your diversification is done for you.

Keep in mind that it is prudent to start slowly and conservatively. As you learn more and gain more confidence your investments can become more aggressive and riskier. To be a successful investor you do not need to "outperform" the stock market, just matching the market will give you substantial affluence and wealth. Remember investing is not gambling. Investing is thoughtful and based on research and education. Gambling is impulsive and based on emotion. Be SELF-FULL. Be thoughtful and wise.

Retirement 101

The third element to SELF-FULL finances is preparing for the future. For most of us that means, planning for our retirement. Coincidentally, one of the easiest ways to get started on your road to SELF-FULL finances is to get your retirement account set up. The sad truth is that those of us coming to age in the early 21st century will not be able to depend on government subsidies such as Social Security and Medicare the way that our grandparents and parents did. We need to be responsible for ourselves in our retirement years. And isn't that better any way? Isn't that the SELF-FULL way to be?

Depending on whether you are self-employed, an employee, or a homemaker, your retirement account will take on a different form. My best advise to you is for you to go the library and pick up a book or two on finance and investing and start reading. Learn the difference between a 401K plan and an IRA. Teach yourself which one you are eligible for and then go to your accountant, bank, or broker and set it up. Then make the maximum contribution you are allowed to make each year. After becoming debt free, make contributing to your retirement your number one financial obligation for the year.

10

SELF-FULL HOBBIES AND INTERESTS

Let's have some fun! A SELF-FULL life is a well-rounded life. It includes healthy relationships, a satisfying professional life, a warm and loving home life and stimulating and entertaining activities. This chapter is about bringing those activities into your life.

Playtime

Have you ever been so engrossed in a activity that you lost all track of time? Have you ever challenged yourself and won? If you have answered no to these questions, boy are you in for a treat! My goal is to introduce you to a whole world of possibility—the world of "arts and leisure."

Let's start with a simple exercise. I call it "What do You Enjoy?"

Exercise. *What do you enjoy?*

Take a few moments to reflect on the activities that you enjoy. Remember back to childhood and those lazy Sunday afternoons or extended summer vacations. How did you fill your days?

1. Make a list of the activities that you have enjoyed in the past.

_____

_____

_____

_____

_____

_____

_____

_____

_____

_____

_____

2. Now, make a list of the activities that you currently enjoy.

_____

_____

_____

_____

_____

_____

_____

_____

_____

_____

_____

3. And, how about the ones that you have been thinking about but have not tried yet.

_____

_____

_____

_____

_____

_____

_____

_____

_____

_____

_____

A major complaint I hear often when I speak with people about adding more activity into their lives is that they don't have the time to do so. Is that true for you too? Actually most of us have more time available for some fun activities than we think. One SELF-FULL way to open up this time is to learn to delegate tasks to others. So many of us are used to doing everything ourselves. Learning to take care of yourself means learning to let go of some of the chores we impose upon ourselves. The next exercise will help you to make some more time, if time is your problem.

Exercise. Time-savers

Here are some ideas for delegating chores so you can create time for yourself. To begin with share household chores with your spouse and family. Create a plan or flow chart where you record who does what. Teach your children to earn their allowance money by raking the yard or walking the dog or throwing out the trash. Next consider hiring someone to do some of your chores for you: get a dog walker, a housekeeper, a student to wash your car or mow your lawn. Also inquire into delivery services. Many dry cleaners and grocery stores will deliver. Catalog shopping is also another great way to save time.

1. What are some things you can do to free up some time for you to enjoy a hobby or interest? Record your ideas here.

_____

_____

_____

_____

_____

_____

_____

_____

_____

_____

_____

2. Now do one! Which one will you do?

_____

_____

_____

_____

_____

_____

_____

_____

_____

_____

A Well-Rounded Life

In creating your SELF-FULL well-rounded life, it is valuable to add a new interest or hobby to your life periodically. I like to use summertime to explore a new sport and wintertime to take a class at a local university. How about you? What can you add to your life to make it more fun? One way to find out about what hobbies, activities and other topics of interest are available to you is to get the catalogs from the adult education classes in your area. You might recall we explored this idea earlier in the SELF-FULL Fitness chapter. These catalogs are packed with classes from apple picking and floral arranging to water-skiing and zoology. Museums and libraries also offer lectures and classes. Get on their mailing lists too. As the catalogs and calendars show up take a look. If something strikes your fancy give it a try. You never know what you might learn or whom you might meet.

Use this space to jot down something that you can try or a mailing list you can get onto to add some spice to your life.

_____
_____
_____
_____
_____
_____
_____
_____
_____
_____
_____

Now do it! Remember your goal is not perfection, it is just to have some fun! And don't be afraid to try these things alone. I find that sometimes I have the most fun when I go to something by myself. I am then free to explore and participate at my own pace without worrying about what my companion is doing or needing.

11

SELF-FULL SPIRITUALITY

I debated for a little while about whether to include a chapter on spirituality in this book. My concern was that the subject might turn some people away from the ideas presented in other chapters by labeling me as "new age" or something along those lines. But, I couldn't help thinking about all the work that so many people are doing with respect to their spirituality that I decided to not include it would be to deny a very important aspect of some people's lives. Choosing to have a spiritual life is an individual decision just as deciding on whether to marry or have a child is. Consequently, I want to present some ideas to you to help you make a SELF-FULL decision as to what role spirituality will or will not play in your life.

I am reminded of a conversation I had with a patient. This woman, Molly, was raised in a religious household. She was having difficulty reconciling the psychological growth she was experiencing because of our work together with her religious upbringing. We discussed how the two perspectives were not necessarily diametrically opposed to each other. They could in fact complement each other. I encouraged her to decide her religious practice and her spiritual belief for herself, regardless of the influence of her family. Since that time Molly has embraced a spiritual life that includes regular attendance at a progressive church near her home and continues her regular participation in group and individual therapy.

I encourage you to do the same as Molly—to decide for yourself what role religion and spirituality will play in your life. You decide what you believe and what is important to you. Up until now many of you have merely followed in the footsteps of your family or teachers. Now is the time to place your own footsteps. They may be the same as those you are already following or they may be something entirely different. This chapter is designed to assist you in starting your SELF-FULL spiritual journey. I wish you "namaste", an Indian expression for peace and love.

We're Living in a New Age

Fortunately for those of us alive in the new millennium, there is a vast amount of information available about alternative religious and spiritual belief systems for us to explore. There are entire bookstores devoted to this topic. Even the more mainstream bookstores have large sections filled with interesting reading material. I encourage you to start exploring. Read different books. Attend seminars and workshops. Ask yourself some of the "tough" questions. To accomplish this task, I will inspire your thinking with the following exercise.

Exercise. To Be or Not To Be and other Tough Life Questions

1. Do you believe in God or some other "higher power"? If so, describe your God or higher power. If not, describe what beliefs you do hold.

_____

_____

_____

_____

_____

_____

_____

_____

_____

_____

_____

2. Do you believe in an "afterlife"? If you do, describe what you believe it to be. If you do not, describe what you do believe?

_____

_____

_____

_____

_____

_____

_____

_____

_____

_____

3. What are your thoughts and feeling about fate?

_____

_____

_____

_____

_____

_____

_____

_____

_____

_____

4. Do you believe that everything happens for a reason?

_____

_____

_____

_____

_____

_____

_____

_____

_____

_____

5. What spiritual or religious practice do you currently have? Are you satisfied with it? Would you like any part of it be different?

_____

_____

_____

_____

_____

_____

_____

_____

_____

_____

_____

A Time for Exploration

Now that you have taken some time to think about your spiritual or religious life, it is time to explore the options available to you. In the next exercise, you will be asked to list ideas and resources that you can think of to help you in your spiritual quest. Here are some suggestions: Go to your local bookstore and pursue the New Age section. Attend a meditation workshop at a local church. Visit several different synagogues and attend a variety of different services to see if any of them suit you. Listen to spiritual tapes. Take up yoga. What can you come up with?

Exercise. My Spiritual Journey

List 5 ideas or resources to help you begin your spiritual journey.

_____

_____

_____

_____

_____

_____

_____

_____

_____

_____

Now that you have some ideas, slowly investigate them. Allow your spiritual practice to evolve. This is a very personal choice. What you believe and how you practice is all up to you. It is nobody else's business unless you choose to share it with them. With time you may find a community of people who share your beliefs and practice. Having a community like that is a wonderful gift. I hope you find yours. Namaste.

12

SELF-FULL COPING SKILLS

Welcome to the final chapter in your journey to SELF-FULLNESS. By now you are probably feeling better about yourself. You know who you are, what you want, and what you desire. I hope that through this process you have truly become your very best friend.

We will end our journey together by creating a toolbox of skills for you to draw from as the need arises. Some you are already familiar with because they were introduced earlier. Others will be new to you and you will have a chance to practice and develop them. I call these skills SELF-FULL Coping Skills.

Here is a list of the skills in your toolbox: nutritious eating, adequate exercise, healthy social support, staying healthy, feeling your feelings, positive attitudes, action planning, assertiveness, anger management, time management, stress management, conflict resolution, gaining perspective, goal setting, better decision making, rest, relaxation, recreation, and finding a role model.

Each of these skills, or tools, can be called upon in moments of stress or distress. Their purpose is to help you thrive, not merely survive, under stressful conditions. Chronic stress, as we know, involves continuing conflicting problems, such as unemployment or the process of a divorce. Acute stress involves momentary, disruptive changes, such as a death in the family or even a promotion. Stress in whatever form, if left unchecked, will accumulate and lead to strain and burn-out. Master the skills in your toolbox and you can avoid the breakdown that so many people suffer.

SELF-FULL SKILLS

Nutritious Eating

In Chapter Two SELF-FULL Eating, we explored the value of eating a healthful diet. Among the benefits of healthful eating is the ability to deal better with stress. The healthier you are, the stronger you are and the more resilient you can be to life's misfortunes. Work hard to get your eating healthy. It will do more for you than merely prepare you for bathing suit season.

Adequate Exercise

Along with healthful eating comes adequate exercise. Exercise is a great stress reducer. When you are feeling particularly worn out or worn down, take a walk. Get your feet moving and your arms pumping and in about twenty minutes or so you will feel much better.

Incorporating regular exercise into your daily routine is a great antidote for stress. Imagine a glass of water. The glass is you and the water is the stress. Each day life pours more stress, imagine water, into your glass. If water isn't also removed from the glass each day eventually the glass will over flow. Exercise is like a drain on the bottom of the glass. Open the drain and you allow a little bit of water to leave the glass so that as new water is poured in the glass will not overflow. Daily exercise will reduce your stress so that new stress won't overtake you. Make daily exercise a part of your life.

Healthy Social Support

The next coping skill for your toolbox is having a healthy, strong, and available social network that you can count on in times of need. Take time to develop relationships that offer assistance, security, satisfaction, understanding, respect and encouragement.

Create your own personal support network. Yours might include family members, friends, co-workers, your pastor or rabbi, your therapist, and a reliable dog walker.

Exercise. Weaving Your Net

1. Do you have a support network you can rely on? If so, who is in it?

_____

_____

_____

_____

_____

_____

_____

_____

_____

_____

_____

2. Who is missing?

_____

_____

_____

_____

_____

_____

_____

----

3. If you do not have a support network, what do you need to do to create one? Who will you include? For help getting started, see the discussion on SELF-FULLNESS and the Community in Chapter Four.

Staying Healthy

Like healthful eating, staying healthy is one of your greatest stress fighters. The healthier you are the better able you are to deal with stress because you will have your physical capabilities available to you. Chapter Five on SELF-FULL Health is full of ways for you to improve yours.

In spite of their common usage as a "coping mechanisms", smoking, recreational drug use, overeating, and drinking do not relieve stress. They add to the problem. Not only are you not dealing with the problem that is causing you the stress in the first place, you are also adding an additional stress to your life, namely, a toxic bad habit.

Review the section in Chapter Five on breaking bad habits to help you get rid of yours.

Feeling Your Feelings

This is one of my favorite coping skills, feeling your feelings. Feelings are like waves. If unimpeded, waves will wash over and then recede. If you prevent them from flowing, they will crash against the shore and do considerable damage. Feelings will do the same. Allow yourself the experience of feeling your feelings. They will not hurt you. They will come, wash over you, and recede. You have nothing to be afraid of.

There are many ways to feel your feelings. One way is to sit down and experience them. Let them fill you up and pass through you. And they will pass. Many people are afraid of their feelings because they are afraid that if they let themselves feel they will forever feel bad. It's not true. The sooner you allow yourself to have the feeling, the shorter its duration and the quicker it will pass. If sitting with your feelings is uncomfortable, then write them down or talk with a friend, counselor, or into a tape recorder. Whichever method you choose, merely feel your feelings, you do not have to act on them.

Exercise. *I've Got a Feeling*

1. When was the last time you felt a feeling? What feeling was it? How did it "feel?"

_____

_____

_____

_____

_____

_____

_____

_____

_____
_____
_____

2. What did you do to express your feelings?

_____
_____
_____
_____
_____
_____
_____
_____
_____
_____

3. What was the outcome of expressing your feelings?

_____
_____
_____
_____
_____
_____
_____
_____
_____
_____

4. The next time a feeling comes over you, what are you going to do?

_____

_____

_____

_____

_____

_____

_____

_____

_____

_____

Positive Attitudes

A positive attitude is another tool to managing stress and coping with life. When you learn to have a positive attitude about yourself and your life, things get better.

The first component to a positive attitude is positive thinking. Positive thinking means teaching yourself to expect the best, instead of the worst. It means looking for what's right in a situation rather than dwelling on what is wrong. As cliché as it sounds, being a positive thinker is the number one way to take charge of your life.

You are constantly talking to yourself. Your mind is chattering away even when you are not paying attention. What kind of thoughts are filling your mind? Are you saying positive life affirming statements or is your head filled with negative, catastrophizing thinking?

What you say to yourself can go a long way in how you feel about yourself. Your self-image and your life is determined by your inner dialogue. Practice filling your head with positive statements. Practice seeing what is right about you instead of what you can't stand.

One way to do that is through a technique called "thought stopping". Thought stopping is a method of catching yourself in the middle of a negative thought and immediately replacing it with a positive one.

Exercise. Thought Stopping

1. Close your eyes for a moment and pay attention to your inner dialogue. What is it saying? Are the comments positive or negative? Write down what you are thinking here.

_____

_____

_____

_____

_____

_____

_____

_____

_____

_____

2. If your inner dialogue was negative, rewrite the script here replacing the negative thoughts with positive ones. For example, let's pretend that your mind was filled with thoughts of how fat you are and how unattractive you feel. Replace those harsh negative thoughts with thoughts such as, "I am working hard to improve my eating habits and soon I will be slim and feel more attractive."

_____

_____

_____

_____

_____

_____

_____

_____

_____

_____

3. Each time you catch yourself thinking a negative thought, replace it immediately with something else. After a little while you will automatically be thinking more positively. Record the changes you experience here.

_____

_____

_____

_____

_____

_____

_____

_____

_____

_____

_____

Action Planning

Action is a simple and effective antidote for depression and anxiety. Doing something, anything, can get you out of the dumps and into recovery.

If you are in a bad place in your life, start scheduling your days. Fill it with anything you can think of doing. Get a day planner or another calendar of some sort and plan every hour of the day. You don't have to do it all, just start "doing it!" The action alone will make things better.

Exercise. Lights, Camera, Action!

1. Make a list of all the things you can do to keep yourself busy.

_____

_____

_____

_____

_____

_____

_____

_____

_____

_____

_____

2. Keep your list handy so you can reach for it the next time you are in the dumps and need a "quick fix." Where will you keep your list?

_____

_____

_____

_____

_____

_____

_____

_____

_____

_____

_____

Assertiveness

Saying NO! without guilt and in a way people respect is the epitome of assertiveness. You were trained in assertiveness in Chapter Four.

Continue to develop your assertiveness so it becomes one of the strongest skills in your repertoire.

Anger Management

Anger is sometimes described in psychological circles as an unmet wish. Something you wished had occurred that did not. For example, Sarah wanted her husband to bring her flowers on Friday nights. When he did not she got angry with him. The unmet wish was that her husband would care enough about her to bring her flowers. Because he failed to do so, the wish went unmet. To address this unmet wish, Sarah spoke with her husband about her feeling that she is uncared for. She explained to him that his bringing her the flowers each week would tell her how much he cared. Once her husband understood Sarah's unmet wish and realized how far a simple gesture such as bringing Sarah flowers could go to improve the quality of their marriage, he gladly brought them to her. Since then, Sarah's dinner table has been adorned with flowers every Friday night.

What are your unmet wishes? They are at the root of your anger. If you can identify the unmet wish in a particular situation you will be able to resolve your anger more easily.

Exercise. Unmet Wishes

1. Recall a time in your life when you felt especially angry. Describe in detail what the circumstances were.

_____

_____

_____

_____

_____

_____

_____
_____
_____
_____

2. Looking back at that event, can you identify what wish of yours went unmet? Describe your unmet wish.

_____
_____
_____
_____
_____
_____
_____
_____
_____
_____
_____

3. What could you have done then, or what can you do now, to satisfy that wish?

_____
_____
_____
_____
_____
_____
_____
_____
_____
_____
_____

Time Management

Each of us only has twenty-four hours in any given day and yet some of us manage to get lots of tasks done and others can't do much at all. What is the difference? Time management. Time management is learning to make the most of the time you've got. Being efficient and doing things only once are two specific time management skills.

In Chapter Ten, SELF-FULL Hobbies and Interests, there is an exercise called *Time-savers*. Take a look at that exercise again and see if you can incorporate some more time-savers into your life.

Stress Management

What is stress? Stress, quite simply, is the way you react to change. Your reactions can be physical or emotional. If your reactions are negative you can end up with health or other problems. So what can you do to react positively to the stress in your life? Here are some SELF-FULL steps you can use to make your life go more smoothly.

The first step to managing your stress is becoming aware of the things that make you feel "stressed out." I call these your "personal stressors". One way to identify your "personal stressors" is to listen to your body. It will give you signals that you are heading for trouble. Some of these signals include: headaches, stomach aches, dizziness, heart palpitations, clammy hands, fatigue, tensed muscles, and clenched teeth. Another way is to pay attention to your feelings. Feelings of depression, anxiety, nervousness, helplessness, or hopeless are signals. Make note of when you experience these signals. Notice if there are any patterns to their occurrence. These patterns are your stressors.

The second step in managing stress is learning to deal with your "personal stressors" directly. The techniques in this chapter will help you do just that.

The third step in stress management is learning to relax. This is such an important skill that I have devoted an entire section to its cause.

Exercise. *Stress-busters*

1. What are your "personal stressors?" Traffic jams? Phone calls from telemarketers? A baby crying? Guest arriving late?

_____

_____

_____

_____

_____

_____

_____

_____

_____

_____

_____

2. What signals does your body give off when you are under stress?

_____

_____

_____

_____

_____

_____

_____

_____

_____

_____

_____

3. What could you do to deal with your "personal stressors" sooner and more directly? Some ideas include: avoiding minor hassles; limiting changes; controlling the timing of events; trying not to do too many things at once; taking a break; finding help; and, prioritizing tasks.

_____

_____

_____

_____

_____

_____

_____

_____

_____

_____

Conflict Resolution

Nothing brings more terror to many folks than confrontation. I know people who would do practically anything in order to avoid confrontation. Are you one of those? If you are read, re-read, and read again the section on Assertiveness in Chapter Four.

Another technique to add to those presented in Chapter Four is "rehearsal." Rehearsal is a method of practicing ahead of time what you will say or do in a given situation. This technique is especially helpful for confrontation.

Exercise. Dress Rehearsal

1. Imagine a situation you will encounter when you will need to confront someone. Describe that upcoming confrontation here. Include what you anticipate the other person will say or do in response.

_____

_____

_____
_____
_____
_____
_____
_____
_____
_____
_____

2. Now pretend you are a lawyer preparing a witness to testify. You are also the witness. Gather all your information and write out answers to questions that the other person might pose to you.

_____
_____
_____
_____
_____
_____
_____
_____
_____
_____
_____

3. Rehearse out loud what you will say to the other person when you see them. Practice until you feel confident. You could rehearse in front of a mirror, with a tape recorder, or with a friend. When and how will you rehearse?

_____
_____
_____

_____

_____

_____

_____

_____

_____

_____

_____

Gaining Perspective

Moving on to the next SELF-FULL coping skill in your toolbox, gaining perspective. Sometimes when we are in the middle of a crisis or dilemma we lose the "forest for the trees." Gaining perspective is a helpful tool for putting things in order and becoming more objective.

To gain perspective do the following. First gather more information. Try to see the whole picture and where your problem fits in. Second, identify your options. Recognize that there may be more than one way to view your problem and more than one solution. Third, weigh the costs and benefits of each option you identified. And, lastly, evaluate the situation realistically. Try to keep your emotions out of it, if you can.

Goal Setting

Successful goal setting is mastered by setting small attainable goals and consistently pursuing them. Most people fail at their goals because they make their goals too lofty. Often these people smirk at the idea of setting small goals because they think "I can do more than that," or "If I set small goals, it will take too long to get where I want to go." I ask, "Where are these people now?" Chances are they are nowhere near meeting their goals. Chances are they abandoned their goal setting efforts. If they had set small steps and pursued them consistently they would be far along their goal setting path. Remember every journey begins with a first step. I have been known to say, the time is going to pass anyway so why not spend your time working on your goals. This way when the year or decade has passed, and it will, you have something to show for it besides a worn out calendar!

Here is a goal setting secret that is as important if not more important than setting small goals. The secret is to write down your goals. People who write down their goals are more successful than those who just think about their goals or just "wish" about them.

Starting right now, write down your goals. Here's how. You begin by setting a large goal, such as losing 20 pounds. Then you break that goal into small sub-goals. For example, lose 5 pounds, then 10 pounds, then 15 pounds. Then you break you sub-goals into even smaller goals. For example, one pound at a time. And you go for it!

Exercise. Goal For It!

1. Write down a goal you would like to achieve this year.

_____

_____

_____

_____

_____

_____

_____

_____

_____

_____

2. Divide your goal into six-month, three-month and one-month sub-goals.

_____

_____

_____
_____
_____
_____
_____
_____
_____
_____
_____

3. Write down the action you will take today to reach your one-month sub-goal.

_____
_____
_____
_____
_____
_____
_____
_____
_____
_____
_____

4. When this goal is met, set another one. What will your next goal be?

_____
_____
_____
_____
_____
_____

_____

_____

_____

Better Decision Making

Decisions based on fact are better than those based on hunches or whims. Sleeping on a decision is good advice. If is still sounds good in the morning, then it is probably a good idea.

To make a better decision, you need to start with your "outcome." What exactly is it that you want to achieve? Then measure each choice against that outcome. Ask yourself, "will this choice move me closer to or father way from my outcome?" Choose the choice that moves you closer and you will have made a better decision.

Exercise. Building a Better Mouse Trap

1. What decision are you struggling with?

_____

_____

_____

_____

_____

_____

_____

_____

_____

_____

2. What is the outcome you want to achieve?

_____

_____

_____

_____

_____

_____

_____

_____

_____

_____

_____

_____

3. Describe your option(s).

_____

_____

_____

_____

_____

_____

_____

_____

_____

_____

4. Does your option(s) move you closer to or farther way from your outcome?

_____

_____

_____

_____

_____

_____

_____

_____

_____

_____

_____

3 R's : Rest, Relaxation, and Recreation

Remember the 3R's from grammar school—reading, writing, and arithmetic? Well, now I will introduce you to 3 new R's—rest, relaxation and recreation.

Rest

Rest can take many forms. It can be a catnap in the middle of the day. It can be turning the phone off and putting your feet up. It can be a warm, soothing cup of tea. It can be lying on the couch and reading your favorite novel. It can also be getting a good night's sleep. Whatever manner of rest you choose, make certain you choose it often. Rest is a vital part of a SELF-FULL life.

Exercise. Rest Remedies

1. What manner of rest will you incorporate into your SELF-FULL life?

_____

_____

_____

_____

_____

_____

_____

_____

_____

_____

Relaxation

You can break the cycle of stress in your life by learning ways to relax. Pamper yourself with massages, saunas, Jacuzzis, and bubble baths. There are also several relaxation techniques that you may find helpful. By taking the time to practice some of them, you will go a long way to managing your stress and your life.

The first technique is called "Clearing Your Mind". To clear your mind, find a comfortable place to sit. Reduce distractions by turning off the phone and closing the windows. Next, mentally focus on one thought, word, or image. Breathe comfortably and enjoy your peaceful mind.

The second technique is called "Progressive Relaxation." To use this technique, again reduce distractions. Lie comfortably and close your eyes. Tighten the muscles in your feet. Hold for a count of ten. Release. Continue up your body tightening up each muscle group as you go. When you are finished, lie quietly and enjoy your tension-free body.

The third technique is "Light Stretching." Stand up. Gently stretch your arms over your head and reach your finger tips to the sky. Now stretch your arms out in front of you and reach for the wall. Then reach for the floor. Circle your arms gently in large sweeping movements. Shake out your wrists and arms. Lightly tilt your head from side to side. And, lastly, roll your shoulders forward and back. Are you feeling better now?

Recreation

An important coping skill is having some fun in your life. All work and no play makes Jane an unhappy camper, you know. Chapter Ten, SELF-FULL Hobbies and Interests, was devoted to the idea of adding more fun and recreation into your life. Review that Chapter again to get your recreational juices flowing and then go and have some fun!

Exercise. Girls Just Want To Have Fun

1. What can you do to add more fun and recreation into your life? Jot your ideas down here.

_____
_____
_____
_____
_____
_____
_____
_____
_____
_____

Finding a Role Model

The last SELF-FULL coping skill you will learn is called "Finding a Role Model." Sadly, there are very few heroes for us to emulate, so you have to go out and find yourself one. There are people out there doing what you want to do, living the way you want to live. Find them. Most would be flattered that you find them inspirational and will gladly share their information with you. I hope that through this book I have become a role model of sorts for you. Who could be your role model? Let's find out.

Exercise. Follow the Leader

1. Whom do you admire? Who is doing what you want to do? Living the way to want to live?

_____
_____
_____

_____
_____
_____
_____
_____
_____
_____
_____

2. How can you reach that person? Is she someone you know who you could call or write? Is he a celebrity who is unapproachable? Or perhaps the person has died? If the person is unreachable, how can you learn more about them and their life? Was there a book written about them or a movie?

_____
_____
_____
_____
_____
_____
_____
_____
_____
_____
_____

3. If the person is reachable, how will you reach them?

_____
_____
_____
_____

_____

_____

_____

_____

_____

_____

4. If the person is unreachable, what will you do to learn more about them?

_____

_____

_____

_____

_____

_____

_____

_____

_____

_____

_____

THE END OF THE BEGINNING

So, we have now come to the end of our journey together to SELF-FULLNESS. This may mark the end of our time together, but it marks the beginning of the rest of your quest.

I wish you continued success and joy as you become all you can be.

AFTERWORD

I sincerely hope that you found yourself described in these pages and that as a result of reading this book and doing the exercises contained inside that you too are now on your own journey to SELF-FULLNESS. If I can be of any assistance to you in your journey to SELF-FULLNESS, or if you would like to be on my mailing list, please write to me at 2730 Wilshire Blvd. Suite 620, Santa Monica, California 90403

I wish you joy, happiness, success, and an abundance of SELF-FULLNESS.

Sheila H. Forman, J.D., Ph.D.

ABOUT THE AUTHOR

Sheila H. Forman. J.D., Ph.D. is both a licensed clinical psychologist and attorney, earning degrees from the Johns Hopkins University and Boston University. She divides her time between a private clinical practice in Santa Monica, California specializing in women's issues, particularly self-esteem, anxiety, and depression and teaching graduate level psychology students subjects including law, ethics, practice development, group psychotherapy and eating disorders. She is also a certified group psychotherapist registered in the National Registry of Group Psychotherapists.

TABLE OF EXERCISES